Quite
Quintessential

Also by Jeremy Cameron

Never Again
A Walk from Hook of Holland to Istanbul

Quite Quintessential

A Walk Round the Qs of England

[signatures: Jeremy Cameron]

JEREMY CAMERON

Signal

Signal Books
Oxford

First published in 2019 by
Signal Books Limited
36 Minster Road
Oxford OX4 1LY
www.signalbooks.co.uk

A catalogue record for this book is available from the British
Library

ISBN 978-1-909930-77-3 Paper

Cover Design: Alice Mara & Tora Kelly
Typesetting: Tora Kelly
Cover Image: Alice Mara
Printed in India by Imprint Press

Day 1: Westacre to Ashill
(11 March)

The Nar Valley Way runs past my door. Upstream it leads to Castleacre, popular village and tourist attraction. In Castleacre it meets Peddars Way, ancient Roman road which takes me all the way to my destination for the day. There is no need to meet motorised traffic at all and it's a lovely walk.

So I didn't do any of that. I walked straight down the road; it was shorter and I wouldn't get lost. Peddars Way may be the straightest route in the world; it leads directly across the map. I could still get lost on it.

There was another factor. It was bitterly cold. The forecast last night said it would be bitterly cold. It was right. It was way below zero and the wind made it minus seven. From time to time it snowed. For variety we had a shower of hail. I entered Ashill in a blizzard.

Fifty years ago, my father used to walk the five miles from Westacre to Swaffham on a Sunday morning. After a glass of beer at The George, my mother would pick him up and drive him home for lunch. On Fridays too, all the farmers would gather in The George at lunchtime. Then they would go to the bank and pick up the cash for the men's wages, distributed in pay packets on Friday afternoon. Now there are three men on the farm where there used to be forty, and they don't get paid in cash.

After a month's rainfall in twenty-four hours at the weekend, the River Nar was coursing through the village. Up on Swaffham Hill someone was having a bonfire of hedge trimmings on the Forty Acres; most of the fields have names but this one is just the Forty Acres over the River. It was cold. On this road you see deer, weasels, hares and owls. I saw none of them today. They stayed indoors.

In Swaffham I bought fruit and nuts for the birds and for me and two books in Ceres Bookshop just for me. In the Pedlars Hall Café I had tea and a large piece of Victoria cake. The woman in charge said she would stay in the warm if she were me. I pushed on down the back road to Ashill.

Today is just a loosener, eleven miles to see how the joints are working. Ashill is about halfway to Quidenham, my first destination. It's also where Barbara and Syd live.

I rang them last night and asked if they would bring me back home if I cooked them a meal in exchange. Instead they fed and watered and wined me in Ashill, then brought me home into the bargain. If someone was to bring me home after every stage of this walk it would be perfect. By nine o'clock I was sitting in front of the fire watching TV. I will go back and carry on as soon as possible.

Some people have asked me why I am walking to all the places beginning with the letter Q. The answer, of course, is obvious: why not?

Q

In 1970 I walked from London to Villach in southern Austria. In 1972 it was Quebec City to Detroit, in 1973 Athens to Peć in what is now Kosovo. In 1980 I walked from New York to California, while 1984 was London to Split. 1990 (I think – I get a bit vague about later years) I went from Managua in Nicaragua through Honduras (wild) to Guatemala City. In 1997 I walked from Agra through Delhi to Chandigarh, following the path of the cricket World Cup (although, inconveniently, they didn't schedule all the matches in a straight line). Some time after that, realising I was too old for the continuous venture, I walked intermittently from London to Venice. (Walk a few days, come home, go back and walk another few days.) A couple of years ago, thinking I wasn't too old after all, I managed Hook of Holland to Istanbul. Never again. I am much too old. What next therefore? The only possible option was to walk round all the places in England beginning with the letter Q.

It's surprising that no-one has done it before. Why has no-one wanted to see whether they have anything in common, these places starting with Q? And has no-one investigated the people? What are they like? Are they querulous? Are they queasy? Queer? Quaint? Quavery? Or queenly? Do they quest a lot? Or are they simply quiescent? Above all, what is it like to live somewhere that begins with the letter Q? It is my mission to find out.

I have always avoided walking in England. It's far too dangerous. On roads in almost every other part of the world there are nice wide verges where you can get well out of the way of the oncoming traffic, but in England you are reduced to hugging the hedges on crazy blind corners. As for footpaths, they aren't generally in good shape and you instantly get lost. But I don't want to go abroad again. I've had enough of abroad. I can't get a proper newspaper every day and, it has to be said, they don't speak English. It is a real pleasure to walk into a café and get what you ask for without having to repeat yourself because you don't pronounce 'tea' correctly. Furthermore, you can actually get a real cup of tea.

Finally, I intend to go home at night whenever possible. It may be necessary to stay away from time to time, but not if I can help it. In addition, I intend to call on (unsuspecting) people I know whenever it is convenient for me. So I shall begin by walking from my house to Quidenham, go home then return and walk from Quidenham to Queen Adelaide, then again to Quendon, and so on. It should keep me out of mischief for a while. There seem to be places beginning with Q all over the country, between forty and fifty altogether.

I bought a book of road maps, supplemented by a map of waterways (canals - great for walking along) and a clutch of Ordnance Surveys in case I really do have to walk along footpaths. If a Q is in the book of road maps, I will try to walk there. If it's not, you can forget it. People keep telling me about some obscure hamlet near them that begins with Q but I'm not interested. Nor will I go somewhere hyphenated that doesn't begin with Q - Somewhere-Cum-Quy, for example. One has to draw the line.

So that was Day 1.

Day 2: Ashill to QUIDENHAM (nearly)
(15 March)

It's my birthday! Sixty-six today. Clickety click. And what better way to spend it than walking to somewhere beginning with Q?

Colin dropped me in Ashill to carry on where I left off.

It was in Ashill, incidentally, that Derek Curl and I shared a tough stand in an epic cup match against Jentique in about 1967. In those days, Ashill had a cricket ground; now it has totally disappeared. Derek and I came together, in a low scoring match, with eighteen needed to win.

'We'll get 'em in singles, Derek,' I said.

Derek may not have known that this is what George Hirst said to Wilfred Rhodes in another epic match, the fifth test against Australia in 1902. 'We'll get 'em in singles, Wilfred.' They needed fifteen to win, the last pair together.

Hirst and Rhodes got 'em. So did Derek and I.

We still reminisce about those days, two old men together. Derek once hit a ball over the road at Westacre and into the Methodist chapel beyond. While we all went off to look for it, play started again with another ball. Suddenly a cry went out: 'Look up!' Derek hit the next ball into the chapel as well.

From Ashill I picked up Peddars Way at Little Cressingham and followed it into Breckland. This was once a huge area of thousands of acres of bracken covering sparsely populated open land. Was that a curlew I saw, was that a peewit? Once there were peewits (lapwings) everywhere but now they are mostly gone. Masses of yellowhammers fluttered round the hedges and a couple of green woodpeckers scarpered by. Then the path entered forbidden territory.

During the Second World War, the government appropriated a large section of Breckland for battle training. Villages were emptied of their residents, who were told they would return at the end of the war. When the end of the war came, they were told they couldn't. Periodically since then, the dwindling survivors have been allowed back on visits to see briefly their old homes: visited but never permanently lived in again.

During the 1950s my parents were friends with Godfrey Rampling and his wife Anne. Godfrey, a permanent soldier stationed at the battle area, was famous for his immortal winning leg for Britain in the 4 x 400 metres relay (or was it 4 x 440 yards?) at the 1936 Berlin Olympics. To us he was just a friend of my parents. He also had two lovely daughters, of whom Charlotte became rather well known.

Now Peddars Way runs for miles along the wire that borders the battle area. From the right, war was being waged in an eruption of gunfire: small arms, machine guns and then huge explosions. It made you want to dive headlong and wriggle on your belly. Instead, locals took their dogs for peaceful walks. I was heading for the pub at Wretham for lunch.

It was shut. There are few things more disappointing in life than a shut pub.

Speaking of pubs, I had bought a book about Peddars Way. At least, I thought I had. Instead, it turned out to be a book about pub crawls in the vicinity of Peddars Way. If I had noticed this earlier I might have saved a lot of time. Pressing blindly on instead of forking left, the path took me miles away from the route to Quidenham. Eventually I found the road through Bridgham to East Harling. By this time I had done six hours for the day, enough walking.

A mile from East Harling, a man called Ray stopped to offer a lift; he had seen me three times on the road and wondered if I was heading for the Carmelite retreat (I think) and children's hospice at Quidenham, where apparently Sister Wendy appears on TV from time to time. He said there was precious little else in Quidenham but that I could get a cup of tea in East Harling. I explained what I was doing, accepted his kind offer of a lift and assured him I would come back and walk the mile next time. At Harling the landlord of The Swan offered refuge from the rain and a soothing cup of tea.

At the bar, a semi-professional footballer was smoking an electronic cigarette, the one that satisfies the nicotine addiction while omitting the tar. Was it a good idea to be addicted to anything? And was it a good idea to be drinking on the day before a match? ('But they don't know,' he said.) He said the manager was trying to convert him from a striker into a full back although he was only twenty-two. He was a nice lad but perhaps the manager was trying to tell him something about his fitness.

The paper today was full of the visit to Norwich by the new Archbishop of Canterbury. He's got his work cut out here. At the last census, Norwich was officially assessed as the most godless place in the country. Yesterday, a plethora of worshippers descended on the Arch during his visit - but far more people were surveyed who said they didn't care a hoot. It's nice to have the churches and cathedrals but a pity about their contents.

Day 3: QUIDENHAM to Thetford
(23 March)

So what is it like, living in a place beginning with Q?

And are the people querulous and queasy?

Unfortunately I didn't meet anyone in Quidenham to find out. And it was a difficult day.

Spring is here, or so it says on the calendar. The north of England is closed today. Belfast was cut off from electricity altogether last night. Power lines are down, motorways are closed. Fifteen-foot snow drifts have hit the Lake District. The forecast last night said: 'It will be bitterly cold.' In Norfolk, gale force, biting winds are slicing from the east. All day it snowed, rained or sleeted. At the end the snow started to settle. As I finished the day's walking in Thetford, Radio Norfolk broadcast a football report from Thetford. Freezing cold, they said.

The weather was not the major problem, though.

The plan was to drive my car to Eccles Road, walk to Quidenham and then Thetford, catch the train back to Eccles Road and go about my business.

Quidenham has a timber yard which I never saw. It has a hospice away to the left which I never saw. Apparently it has a retreat, separate from the hospice, which I never saw. It has a lot of very comfortable houses; in fact it doesn't have any houses that aren't comfortable. It has a quirky (another Q) church. At first I couldn't identify what was so unusual about it. Then I realised: it has a round, Saxon, normally flat-topped tower, but this one has a spire. The higher you go, of course, the closer to God.

Quidenham was, in fact, quiet. Indeed no-one seemed to be alive there so I headed on to East Harling. That was my first Q!

An estate agent called Kissinger has sold a house in Quidenham. To those of us of a certain age, Kissinger can only mean the bombing of Cambodia. Perhaps it's another Kissinger.

Through flat, straight, open roads the forest led to the main road from Diss. Oh, that wasn't part of the plan. Often I have driven down this road on the way to my sister Sarah's house, but I never contemplated walking along it. A woman in a Volvo stopped and offered a lift, clearly reasoning that only a lunatic would walk down the A1066 in a snowstorm. I politely declined. Past the Shadwell stud, where extremely rich people keep their horses, the road ran on endlessly. To cut a long story short, I missed the train by about five minutes and the next one was forty-two hours later. Yes, forty-two.

Once, on the overland route from Egypt to Sudan, I waited at Wadi Halfa for the train to arrive. No-one knew how long it would be. On that occasion it was fifteen hours, which was thought to be very good. The average wait was three or four days and I met someone who had waited for a fortnight.

Thetford, stuck away in the middle of nowhere, is wildly multi-cultural. I asked for directions from seven or eight people, only two of whom spoke English as a first language. For some reason a Portuguese community has been there for a long time. Now there are many eastern Europeans. One family offered me a lift because I was standing there looking forlorn. Thetford is a poor, deprived town, despite having a priory, a river, The Bell Inn and, according to today's paper, otters. Two police cars cruised endlessly round the town, without anyone ever getting out. I had a cup of tea in Subway.

Day 4: Thetford to Brandon
(25 March)

It was an afternoon world. No, that was just my mistyping from the notebook - very metaphysical. I meant to say that it was an afternoon walk: not much more than three hours. The intention was to walk on to Lakenheath station and catch a train back; but there was a problem. Lakenheath station had no trains.

Trains are shown on the timetable outside the station. This is an active station. However, when you ring for information you meet a wall of silence: it is the call centre person unable to believe her eyes. Yes, Lakenheath has a station, a working station, and you should be able to get on a train there. Yes, trains go along that line and pass through Lakenheath all the time. None of them, however, ever seems to stop.

I confirmed all this with the guard of a train I was on yesterday, a train that actually passed through Lakenheath. He knew his own train didn't stop there but he assumed other trains did. He looked it up. No. No. He scratched his head. Yes indeed, there was a station but nothing ever seemed to stop there.

So he looked up Shippea Hill, the next station down the line. This was even more peculiar. One train per day stops at Shippea Hill, at seven in the morning, heading for Norwich - but no train ever returns! You can go to Norwich but you can't come back again. Shippea Hill is a ghost town. The population has moved, slowly but surely, to Norwich.

I wandered briefly round Thetford, once the capital of East Anglia; my trade union still holds East Anglia branch meetings there. It has a history. It's on the Icknield Way (I think). Many serious people have lived here over the centuries. So who is represented in the statue by the river? Captain Mainwaring!

Dad's Army was filmed nearby. A Dad's Army museum brings the punters to Thetford, allowing them to bathe in fairly harmless nostalgia. My sister Susan had a part in *Dad's Army* at one time but I didn't look to see if she was in the museum.

Q

The man in the tourist office said the footpath by the Little Ouse would take me all the way to Brandon.

A Muntjac deer preceded me into the woods.

You wouldn't think it was possible to get lost on a footpath beside a river and a railway line. For a long while, past the power station and into the forest, the path and I were in accord; then we didn't see each other again. A bridleway led beside the railway line and took me on a major detour round a huge factory on the outskirts of Brandon.

In summer, this whole area is one giant play pen. Campsites, picnic places and activity centres litter the forests; there is even a runway for model aircraft. Some Environment Agency workers said there was a bittern downstream but I neither saw nor heard one. Flint knappers used to work here, making arms as well as houses. Churches stood in the woods. All of this has gone now, turned over to forests and leisure. There wasn't much leisure today. It was still perishing cold, floating just above freezing and buffeted by a cruel east wind. Perhaps three hours was enough after all.

Day 5: Brandon to QUEEN ADELAIDE to Ely
(31 March)

It was an interesting week. On Tuesday I had a meeting in Norwich. Wednesday brought a meeting in London. On Thursday it was a meeting in Sheffield. Then the next day, Good Friday, I collected Mimi from Lewes, Sussex, and took her - where? - to Sheffield! But I read a lot of books, which is the main purpose of train travel.

Today I had a Companion.

Furthermore, this was a Companion with computer, tablet, mobile phone (2) and the strong desire to use them all. We also had apps, maps, googles and printouts till they were coming out of your arse. At all stages we (or at least the Companion) were peering at screens and taking due note of everything the technology told us. My Companion led the way. I did as I was told. As well as being about twenty miles long it was a difficult day navigationally and I was happy to bow to modern science. If I had been alone I would probably still be there now.

The Hereward Way runs, according to the information, from Ely to Brandon. Unfortunately it doesn't run from Brandon to Ely. It is incredibly difficult to read a guidebook backwards. In addition, by all accounts there are bridges down and paths vague. We took short cuts which didn't seem very short. It was Easter Sunday and the pubs were full, no doubt celebrating the rise of Christ. We joined them from time to time in their joy.

Brandon, to general surprise, has an affluent area. We walked through it into the wilderness, along the Little Ouse and the railway line. Deer on all sides took little notice of us. Wetlands are being recovered here and the soil changes quite rapidly from sandy Breckland to peaty fens. At Lakenheath station, scene of no trains, we turned left for the couple of miles into Lakenheath village. In the pub I had a pickled egg.

Fenland is the most boring countryside in England. Totally flat, totally open, shredded with the dykes that drain the land, it must drive you mad. Everyone from William the Conqueror onwards has had trouble finding a way across the bogs, rivers and dykes, and we were no different. At Shippea Hill station, another scene of no trains, we sat and ate bananas.

This is not a land without excitement, however. Prickwillow (an interesting name) contains - wait for it - The Drainage Museum! We had to contain our excitement because it was closed.

Later, a notice on a river read: TROLLING BANNED.

Then: Queen Adelaide!

What can I say about Queen Adelaide, second of the Qs?

Queen Adelaide appears to be below sea level, indeed to have risen quite recently from the depths. It contains three level crossings.

That's about it.

Companion announced that she would be hiding were I to start asking people what it was like to live somewhere beginning with Q. But we didn't see any people. Perhaps there aren't any.

A couple of miles by footpath along the river brought Ely and its big cathedral. The attractive marina and plethora of old buildings make it hard to remember that you have just been walking through England's nastiest countryside. The toilets at the station were out of order. Then the toilet on the train wasn't working. That took the gloss off things.

Day 6: Ely to Waterbeach
(4 April)

Quote:

'The art of not getting bored on walks lies in looking at the same object as yesterday, but thinking something different while you do. Have you noticed the nettles at the fountain outside? I looked at them and thought: they are green, being green is the great merit.

Do you know what I thought yesterday? Nettles can't fly. They are limited.'

I'm reading *Zbinden's Progress* by the Swiss novelist Christoph Simon. I rang Scott, who lives in Basle, and said I would send him the book when I had finished it. 'Don't feel obliged,' he said. He has read bucketfuls of Swiss novelists and apparently is not overwhelmed by them.

Neither the nettles nor anything else is green so far. A howling, freezing gale blew from the north-east. The soil underneath is inundated because of the two-month flood but the soil on top is dry as a bone. Farmers are having to re-plant winter crops; Simon told me he had just ploughed up a field of winter barley because of slugs; tomorrow it will be re-sown with spring barley.

It was flat and it was cold but it didn't last long. I was on the way back from London to Norfolk so just stopped off to do a few miles. From Ely the Fen Rivers Way follows the Ouse and then the Cam through reclaimed wetlands: it's strange that, hundreds of years ago, they drained the fens, but now they're un-draining them again.

Birds of all descriptions sat on the water. On the land too: I counted seventy seven swans on one field, no doubt devouring what is left of the crop. Dykes, rivers, lakes, locks and sluices separate the arable land. The Five Miles from Anywhere inn was a temptation to be resisted. Overshooting Bottisham Lock, I doubled back and had to run through the streets of Waterbeach, an undignified sight, to catch the train. On the platform a waiting woman said Waterbeach was a nice place and that the American air base closed down last week.

Day 7: Waterbeach to Cambridge
(7 April)

Only six miles! At this rate I will be doing this for the rest of my life. There were mitigating circumstances.

No longer the flat, bleak, unresponsive fenlands, this was the flat, bountiful, academic approaches to Cambridge, personified in the cycle path that led the whole way to the city.

Cycle paths are good and bad. On the good side, they are there and they are flat, even, paved and direct. On the bad side, they are full of cyclists. I like cycle paths. I hate cyclists. Yes, I know they are environmentally sound and are fit, friendly, nutritious and all the rest. They are also rude, sanctimonious, often illegal and frequently dangerous. And they get in my way.

Cambridge was also full of Sunday afternoon walkers, generally intellectual looking types, enjoying the beginning of what may really be spring. The river was stacked with boats: rowing eights for men and women, cruisers hired for the holidays, big boats carrying leisurely diners and houseboats full of their owners. These houseboats line canals and rivers all over England. I don't know anyone who owns a boat. Who are these people?

Cambridge arrived gently. It is a comfortable town in which the inhabitants are generally sheltered from the world. A few years ago, an antiquarian bookseller told me that one of his customers, a don from one of the colleges, came in to his shop two or three times each day. Ostensibly he came to see if anything new had come in. Actually it was to make sure that everything was still there. These are the concerns of Cambridge.

But it is comfortable and it is beautiful. I had a cup of tea in the Arts Picturehouse, where it was very, very tempting to stop and see a film. Soon afterwards I wished I had done.

This was supposed to be halfway for the day. Past a few colleges I headed off, over Parker's Piece and down to the station to check the times of the trains back from Shelford, the target for the day. Oh dear. I bought a ticket for today back from Shelford and asked the ticket seller if the trains were running normally. Yes, he said. Then I looked at the timetable. There weren't any.

He had sold me a ticket for today, despite their being no trains today...

Mind you, it was only £1.80. Nevertheless, I didn't feel like spending the night in Shelford without my toothbrush so I threw the ticket in the bin and went home.

Outside the football at Norwich yesterday, a bunch of our club cricketers were talking about one member who keeps getting speeding convictions. He has had six or seven of them. He never goes at more than 40 mph. Unfortunately he never goes at less than 40 mph either. Motorway or town centre, he drives at 40 mph. So, when he is in the town centre, he gets nicked. Then he gets nicked again.

Elsewhere a teenager, working for his dad, claimed four hours' overtime when he had worked only two. Why? 'It felt like four hours,' he said.

Day 8: Cambridge to Great Chesterford (11 April)

It was quite nostalgic. The route ran first down Brooklands Avenue, where we used to hold national meetings of the left-wing pressure group within the trade union. Then it skirted Cambridge University Press, where meetings of the Anglian tennis league took place thirty years ago. As it happened, I was in Oxford yesterday. That was cosy too. Put together, the cities could persuade you that all was well with the world.

The Cambridge Ramblers have invented the West Anglian Way, a footpath running from Cambridge to

London. Their paper directions are excellent, which makes up for the dearth of signposts at ground level. They took me down Hobson's Conduit into the country, past some rather manly allotments and through a wood. Outside the city, everything has changed with the new fixed bus tracks and the endless expansion of Addenbrooke's Hospital. The railway line, however, runs due south. Follow it and you won't go far wrong.

Addenbrooke's is the most wonderful, terrifying hospital in the world. Twice I have visited Fiona there after her terrible operations. Moved by seeing the place at close quarters again, I rang her in the evening. She and Howard will join me for lunch on my next day out.

In Great Shelford I had a cup of tea in The Tree pub. In Sawston I had another. In Ickleton I bought snacks in the village shop. There is a danger of eating too much through trying to support the local community. I can't see a village shop or a café or a pub without buying something.

In The Tree they were talking about staffing at the local Health Centre and the final of *Mastermind*.

These are lovely villages: Sawston, Duxford and Ickleton are full of houses worth hundreds of thousands. There is a puzzle though. If you were going to spend this much money, why would you spend it on a house surrounded by motorways?

Ickleton, the nicest of all, bisects the motorways; at all times the hum of traffic permeates the air. Duxford village lies just across the motorway from Duxford air base, now part of the Imperial War Museum. It is far from an idyllic retreat. Then between Hinxton and Ickleton stands the huge Wellcome Genome Campus, whatever that is. By the banks of the Cam, this is a major industrial base.

All these East Anglian airfields were built in the Second World War. Picture the crews going down the local pub at night, drinking themselves silly and singing round the piano, before going out at five next morning to get killed. Most of them did.

Day 9: Great Chesterford to QUENDON to Bishop's Stortford
(13 April)

Early in the morning, the train from King's Lynn was full of Norwich City supporters going to Arsenal. I should have been there. Even better, you could make a day of it by continuing to Trafalgar Square for the celebrations of Margaret Thatcher's death. But I was glad I didn't go to the football; we lost, following a hotly disputed penalty.

Howard and Fiona joined me for lunch in Newport; in fact they bought me lunch. We talked, of course, about Thatcher. *Socialist Worker* has printed REJOICE in huge letters across the front page. The Tories naturally approve of her making the rich richer and the poor poorer, not to mention the long-term destruction of the country's traditional industries and infrastructure. But I wonder how they can explain away three things: (i) her support for apartheid; (ii) her support for Pinochet; and (iii) the fact that the Tories themselves got rid of her because everyone hated her. They have airbrushed all of this out.

I abandoned the excellent West Anglian Way because there was a footpath running all the way beside the main road. Hearing that I tried never to walk a yard further than necessary, Fiona said: 'You don't really like walking, do you?'

I had never really thought about it. Perhaps I don't.

Recently there seems to have been a surfeit of walking novels. I have just finished *Zbinden's Progress* and I'm reading *The Unlikely Pilgrimage of Harold Fry* by Rachel Joyce. Then there is *The Unnamed*, by Joshua Ferris, of course, but that is almost too depressing to read. All about someone who abandons all family responsibilities due to a compulsion to go walking. It can't be true to life, can it?

Before Newport stands the magnificently stately Audley End House. (Perhaps the rich aren't so bad after all.) Hereabouts lies the highest point of the region, the equivalent of the continental divide in the United States. To the north, the River Granta runs to the Ouse. To the south, all rivers run to the Thames. It's not quite the same as running to either the Atlantic or the Pacific but it's a milestone of sorts.

QUENDON! Just south of Newport, there it is, the third letter Q. Quendon seems to have cottages and mansions. No-one was on the street except for a couple going into the furniture sale in the village hall. I have still not spoken to anyone who lives in a Q. What are they like?

That was Quendon. Outside the village stands a memorial to a man who lived for forty four years in the woods there. He lived to be seventy-eight so he didn't do too badly.

Wendens Ambo: a name to conjure with. Then, later, there is Ugley. Mind you, Howard and Fiona live in Cockayne Hatley.

Rain fell on Bishop's Stortford and indeed on everywhere else.

Day 10: Bishop's Stortford to Harlow
(14 April)

First, a tale to gladden the heart. Snatching a few hours on a Sunday afternoon, I stood on Seven Sisters station to catch the 13.46 to Bishop's Stortford. But it was cancelled. Then the 14.01 wasn't even mentioned; it might never have existed. The 14.31 was due to hasten to Stansted Airport without stopping for man or beast. Would there ever be another train for me and a few others who wanted to spend our day in Bishop's Stortford?

The man in charge at Seven Sisters heard our plight. 'Let me see what I can do,' he said. 'I'll have a word with the driver. I'll ask if he can make an extra stop at Bishop's Stortford for you. I'll be on the platform at the front of the train. If I whistle, he has agreed. Get on the train!'

He went to the engine, he spoke to the driver and he whistled! We leaped aboard. Whether this unscheduled stop was authorised anywhere else was unclear but it worked for us.

I am now so slow that it took three hours to walk ten miles. My feet dragged; I slouch, I trudge, I drag my heels. I can't come again for a week; this is going to take for ever.

But it was pleasant. And very easy. The River Stort runs all the way and beside it is a footpath. Through moorings and marinas, past locks and weirs, along the railway and under the motorway, under the Stansted flightpath, through wetlands and bird sanctuaries and nature reserves, then housing and pubs and factories the river meanders slowly downhill (of course). When my mother was growing up in these parts in the 1920s and 1930s the area was known as the beautiful Hertfordshire/Essex border (Hertfordshire with a silent 't'). It is a very different place now but with some effort you can still think yourself into the past.

The first duckling of the year fluttered around its mother on the water. Has the weather killed off the rest of the brood or was it the usual predators? Ducks are notorious for losing their offspring. I hoped the single duckling would still be around in the morning.

The sun shone.

Day 11: Harlow to Cheshunt
(21 April)

A busy week stopped me coming back earlier. First I had to go to a prison on the Isle of Wight for some work. Then there were tennis meetings. Sarah my sister came round bringing loaves of homemade bread and tubs of homemade jam. I went to the theatre in the village, stealing away at half time (hoping no-one noticed) to watch a programme on TV about George Harrison. Next morning I assisted at a cake stall for the village hall; I was neither use nor ornament in the cake world. The same afternoon Norwich City beat Reading 2-1, an event of heart-stopping excitement and palpitations. So it's back to Sunday on the road to London.

Again my Companion came.

After all the cold, blustery late winter it was a fine day. The population of southern England was out in force, lining the path, basking in the sunshine, drinking tea and eating ice creams. The path still followed the River Stort; indeed it was now a wide cycle path which meant that all those bullying wheelers were out too. The Stort joined the River Lea to become the Lee Valley Park. (Apparently the word Lea, spelled that way for centuries, is too difficult for the twenty-first century.) Boats swirl back and forth. Birds flock. Again we were told that there might be a bittern; I'll believe that when I see it. Pylons sizzle overhead; this is an industrial area. Harlow went. Cheshunt came. That was it.

My right foot is mottled red and purple. I am losing the biggest three toenails and two of the toes are scarlet. It seems worse than usual. An excuse for a rest?

Day 12: Cheshunt to Walthamstow
(24 April)

Now this was a real journey into the past.

Past the White Water Centre, fresh from the Olympics, the River Lea strolls through industry, housing and dual carriageways towards the Thames. I left it to sidetrack through Chingford, home of the lesser, and almost invisible, River Ching.

Chingford has other characteristics beside its river. Friends of mine eventually had to leave Chingford because they knew, without a shadow of doubt, that they would never in their lifetime vote for a winning parliamentary candidate. Chingford thinks hanging and flogging is too soft. Chingford is the land of the aspiring. Aspiring to what? Aspiring to the opposite of whatever they have left behind.

Nevertheless, when I worked in Walthamstow Probation Office we had customers, sometimes many of them, from Chingford. Oh, the nostalgia of walking down the streets where my clients lived! King's Head Hill, Peel Close, College Gardens. Past the cemetery; is this the one where the Krays are buried? Down Chingford Mount, past the Walthamstow dog track (now closed), through the subway under the Crooked Billet Roundabout and into Walthamstow itself.

Walthamstow is home to the longest street market in Britain. Home to - what else? A hundred and fifty languages are spoken in Walthamstow. Then there is the William

Morris Gallery, the Vestry House Museum and Walthamstow village. According to Harry Thompson, author of *This Thing of Darkness*, Charles Darwin brought indigenous people from Patagonia to be 'civilised' in Walthamstow. And it is home, above all, to Walthamstow Probation Office, beside the enormous, beautiful, brutalist Town Hall.

I walked past my old office window, peered inside, couldn't see anything. The very few people who still remember me weren't in evidence. The court has gone, victim of a thousand cuts. For a while I wallowed in memories. I worked here for eighteen years, the focal point of my professional life. There is no point in reflecting all night though. I walked up the hill to have a cup of tea with my grandchildren.

A health warning had been issued on this front. Cora has a stomach bug which, according to repute, could lay you spectacularly low. I risked it. So far, all is well. Tim, Phoebe and their parents Em and Dave were pleased to see me.

In the next couple of days I have to go to Worcester for some work and stay in - let's say one of a well-known cheap chain of hotels. Last time I was there I had just walked in the door to Reception when a small, portly middle-aged man emerged from the lift, wearing nothing but a very brief pair of underpants. 'That girl!' he cried. 'She stole all my clothes!' Whatever the transaction between them, it had not ended satisfactorily. For him, anyway. I hope similar entertainment will be laid on again.

Day 13: Walthamstow to City Airport
(3 May)

The country has exploded into colour after the deluge of winter and the permafrost of the late spring. In the countryside, late blossoming rape has coincided with tulips and blackthorn and primroses. In the cities, the flowering cherries have burst into life, the roundabouts spontaneously blooming. At night there are still frosts. By day, a cool sun shines. Perfect conditions to walk through east London.

After a number of delays, this was only a minnow of a day; and I don't know when I can come back again. I keep being given bits of work. Before my next walking day I shall have been to Winchester (twice), Leeds, London, Bristol and Norwich (four times - football and tennis). Half the world is unemployed, the other half has got more work than it wants.

We walked, my Companion and I, from Walthamstow Central through Wood Street to Whipps Cross, then past the beautiful house on The Forest where I lived with Belinda, now owned by other people who have painted the door a bilious blue. From there, the route lay through the gay cruising area where distracted-looking men were striding purposefully back and forth. This led to Hollow Ponds past Snaresbrook Crown Court to the Green Man Roundabout and Aldersbrook Tennis Club, where I have wasted several thousand hours over the last thirty years. No-one was playing. Beyond Wanstead Flats (not flats at all but a huge expanse of green) there can be only one destination: Green Street, the Asian community of shops, restaurants and businesses, a multi-cultural bonanza of colour, clothing and cuisine.

There isn't really any point in coming to east London if you don't go to Green Street. In the best known vegetarian haunt we had some truly excellent plates of varied snacks. Never mind the schedule; never mind the impossibility of walking after all that food. Never mind all those places beginning with Q. It was with considerable sloth that we set off again, past West Ham United FC (the stadium soon to be abandoned), past the excellent Newham Bookshop and into Beckton. City Airport, the centre of the vast reconstruction of Docklands, lies past the University of East London to the right.

The other day I went to the doctor about a spot on my face. He ignored that but he diagnosed, in the course of various enquiries, possible Parkinson's Disease. Now, this would be very inconvenient when I'm trying to walk round the country. He will send me for tests. It is also a possibility that the symptoms are a side effect of my heart medication. Whatever it is, I need to find some way of doing more than ten miles a day or I'll be doing this till I'm eighty.

Day 14: City Airport to Woolwich
(20 May)

After a gap of a fortnight, this was a day of only one hour! I will be a hundred, not eighty, when I complete the task. I will be the only centenarian walking round the Qs.

In the last two weeks I have been to France and Switzerland as well as all those other places. I have been to two hearings, two funerals and one fortieth wedding anniversary; I have looked after one child, watched one football match and played in one tennis match. It's all very distracting.

From Gallions Reach, by the airport, the road led to the Woolwich pedestrian tunnel under the Thames. The tunnel entrance was invisible under a mountain of building work from the Crossrail project. The tunnel itself was deserted; it used to be full and bustling. Why? They have done away with the lifts. There are one hundred and seven steps. That could be the reason.

Walking through the East End, poverty appears all around; then you arrive in south London which makes east London look affluent. Woolwich is poor, indeed, it is dilapidated. Perhaps the arrival of new rail links will improve the opportunities for some of the most disadvantaged people in the country.

I took the DLR to Canning Town, the Jubilee to Stratford and the Overground to Forest Gate before walking to my tennis club to change for the funeral. I was about to catch the 101 to the crematorium but John and Roy, driving past, gave me a lift instead. In the morning three retired probation officers from Nottingham had spotted me on the DLR while on their way to the Docklands Museum. It was a day for reminiscing among old acquaintances.

But such a sad one. Gary was only fifty-seven. Six months ago he had no idea he was ill. Most moving of all was the address given by his wife Sue. Gary was, like Sue and like most of those present, a probation officer. He was blind. He loved birdsong. Apparently he knew them all. After a couple of glasses of wine he could imitate them all too.

Day 15: Woolwich to Bexleyheath
(24 May)

Two days ago, a terrible murder took place on the streets of Woolwich. It has taken up the first six pages of all the newspapers and will do for a long time. Today the place was flooded with police, edgy but quiet. We headed away from the area.

Somehow we had managed to come out without a map, even an A-Z of London, between us. It would be hard to go far wrong though. If the Thames is on the left, you're going the right way. If it's on the right, you might want to think again.

It rained. Sometimes it rained gently, sometimes it rained hard. Taking the scenic route, we passed through the pleasant parks of suburbia and stopped at a superb Turkish café. After only a few miles we came across Bexleyheath station and suddenly knew that this was not a day to be walking.

London is largely behind now. Kent lies ahead.

Q

Good story of the week. Friends from Manchester (Chorlton-cum-Hardy, Manchester 21) have moved to Whissonsett, Norfolk, the back of beyond. God knows why. Anyway, they naturally brought their cats with them - quiet, domesticated, gentle city cats. Suddenly the cats have turned feral - savage, cruel, furious wild animals. They catch anything that moves (including birds - please don't keep cats) and they bring home, dead or alive, moles, voles, shrews, rats and rabbits. Especially rabbits.

Recently they brought home a rabbit that seemed likely to expire imminently. Sian took it from the cat and placed it in a hedge, assuming it would either die or run away. Two hours later it had done neither. Sian rang the vet. He told her to bring it in. She did. The vet gave it antibiotics and two days' B & B (no charge) before telling Sian it was now fully recovered and she could take it home.

So she did. She set it free.

By now it has probably been killed by the cat, which has learned to take no half measures.

Just in case Sian and Howie should seek alternatives for a future scenario, I described for them how to despatch a rabbit.

Day 16: Bexleyheath to Dartford to Gravesend
(31 May)

A few weeks ago I was buying a train ticket from King's Lynn to London, coming back next day. The very experienced booking clerk said, 'I'll give you one to Dartford.'

'No, I just want to go to London,' I said.

'Dartford is cheaper,' he said.

Dartford is on the other side of London but is £7 cheaper. £7!

'How did you find that out?' I asked.

'Oh. I'm always looking for loopholes,' he said. 'When they block that one I'll find another one.'

Meanwhile, somebody, somewhere has not yet noticed that thousands and thousands of people are allegedly travelling from King's Lynn to Dartford. Soon afterwards, I discovered that Downham Market is the same. I don't know how many tickets I have now bought from west Norfolk to Dartford. Today I actually went there.

Going eastward, to the left lay the panoply of modern industrial England. First came the Dartford river crossing; in both directions, bridge and tunnel, miles of traffic had coagulated into a congealed mess. It was followed by the new docklands: power stations and oil refineries, huge cranes and massive container ships. This is Kent, the Garden of England.

The county is also home to two major pilgrimages. The first is Canterbury Cathedral, which has been going for some while. The second is Bluewater shopping centre which is newer. I restricted myself to a sandwich from the Pound Shop in Dartford. (Yes, it cost a pound.)

Forty-three years ago, I spent a night in Gravesend. In those days I could walk from London to Dover in three days. (Now it is more like thirty-three.) The first stop was Gravesend. I asked around for accommodation and was directed to a café that did rooms.

Yes, they had a bed for the night. There was only one condition: I had to leave by seven in the morning when the other tenant would want the bed. He was a night worker.

So I did.

I think they changed the sheets.

It was enough to deter me from staying in Gravesend tonight, even though I'm back tomorrow. I left.

Day 17: Gravesend to Rochester to Gillingham
(1 June)

In Gravesend it was Saturday (actually it was Saturday elsewhere too) and Union Jacks flew all over the town; I don't know why. In the countryside, everything is a month later this summer and it has all come at once. The mayflower has burst out and the rape is still in flower. The corn is barely in ear and the sugar beet is a disaster but the fields, hedges, verges and woods all look spectacular. England in the early summer is an absolute treat, the most beautiful place on earth.

Rochester is a fine town. It has two prisons outside town. Within the town, castle, cathedral and a lot of old buildings fringe the River Medway, which suddenly bursts into a wide estuary. On the bridge, two teenage girls were walking the other way. What were they talking about? Boys, school, music, the political situation? 'The thing about Miss Havisham...,' one said. Miss Havisham? Is this normal?

Ah, there's a Charles Dickens festival.

Rochester is the town of Dickens and now, for three days, he has taken over. The main street is packed with re-enactments and people in costume, stilt walkers, trick cyclists (no, not psychiatrists) and pipe bands (Dickens?) playing 'Scotland the Brave'. Hundreds of spectators watched the fun.

But where are the bookshops? Isn't this the town with second hand bookshops in every block? Where are the collectors, the fusty old shopkeepers?

The answer lies in the charity shops. Oxfam rules. The second hand bookshops are being done away with. Charities which get their premises cheap and their goods free are driving them out of existence.

Through Chatham, site of a sixteenth-century Royal Dockyard, lay Gillingham. Few people know the whereabouts of Gillingham and even fewer people visit. All I know is that Norwich City have transferred a few players to and from its football club (Iwan Roberts, Steve Bruce). It does possess, however, the most amazing train service and a very laconic ticket inspector. He advised on routes to the (at least) six London terminals served by Gillingham with alarming regularity. It's a good place to get away from.

Day 18: Gillingham to Sittingbourne
(17 June)

I should have gone straight down the main road.

The source of the problem was a disastrous piece of map reading. I was indeed in Gillingham, but the place on the map which I thought was Gillingham was in fact Rainham. I was nowhere near where I thought I had got to. No wonder I was met with blank incomprehension when I asked for the road to Upchurch, a village I had earmarked as a short cut. Later in the day I saw signs for Upchurch but by that time it was behind me. I'm sure it's a nice place.

The Saxon Shore Way appeared, disappeared, appeared and disappeared again. A succession of parks and paths led in approximately the right direction and showed commendable environmental spirit. It is a valiant effort, however, to redeem the irredeemable. The Thames Estuary is hideous.

On both sides of the river, oil refineries and power stations dominate the horizon. When the tide is out, it's all one giant mudflat. The papers today are full of the proposal to build an airport on the estuary. Well, on the one hand it would be hard to make the place any uglier than it is already (although it would destroy myriad wildlife). On the other hand, talk of a new airport location completely misses the point. There shouldn't be a new airport at all. Or an old one. People have got to stop flying.

It's like the other story in today's papers. Which side should we sell arms to in Syria? The answer is: well, neither side actually. We shouldn't be selling arms to anyone. We shouldn't be manufacturing arms.

After wandering round for a couple of hours, directed helpfully by various Kentish people, I found myself at Rainham station. From here the solution was clear: get on the A2 and stay on it. It's been a long straight road for thousands of years and no-one from the Romans onwards has ever got lost there. I made good progress - though not good enough to get to the Isle of Sheppey as planned - and took a detour to Sittingbourne, past a lovely cricket ground, to find a station to get out again.

Later this week I'm going to the launch of Elizabeth Gowing's book on Edith Durham; I stayed with Elizabeth and Robert in Kosovo and go to all their launches. This one is being held at Stanfords, the book and map shop in Long Acre. There really won't be any excuse not to have a proper map after that. Reading it, of course, may be another matter.

Day 19: Sittingbourne to QUEENBOROUGH!
(2 July)

It is a moot point whether I am obliged to include Queenborough at all on the list of Qs, since it is on an island and not part of mainland England. There is, however, a bridge which one can walk over, so conscience dictates having a go.

The Isle of Sheppey is one of the most desolate places in the kingdom. Years ago, I used to come here to visit the three prisons: Elmley, Standford Hill and Swaleside. It was a forbidding journey into a nether world, made worse by never being able to get any lunch near the prisons. Sheppey is apparently a great place for birds. Good.

Q

I had a client once who came out of Standford Hill on parole. He was an East End wide boy for whom things normally worked out (except this once). When he was released on parole he asked if he could go to work in Spain.

'Well,' I said. 'I can tell you what will happen. I have to apply to the Home Office on your behalf. I will support your application. They will say no.'

Which was exactly what happened. It was stupid because he had proof of work to go to, but the Home Office had a policy of turning everyone down regardless.

'Now,' I said to him. 'I want to see you every two weeks on the dot. I will send your reminder to your address a few days beforehand. OK?' The address was in Chingford.

'Yes,' he said. 'OK.' We both knew what was going to happen. He was going to Spain whether he had permission or not.

I sent all his reminders and he kept all his appointments. We chatted, avoiding awkward subjects like where he got his sun tan.

At Christmas, he gave me a bottle of wine.

'Thank you,' I said. 'I am not allowed to accept gifts except for a token where it would be hurtful to refuse. Therefore I will gladly accept this token. Another time, though, I would appreciate it if the gift did not come in a duty free bag from Madrid airport.'

'Oh,' he said. 'Sorry.'

It was the only mention either of us made of Spain throughout his parole. He completed the period without incident, another success for the Probation Service and a criminal who did not trouble the people of Britain.

Q

From Sittingbourne, I made my way through Iwade to Sheppey. At one time, you always got held up by traffic on the bridge and you were late for your prison visit. Now they have built a great big swirling dual carriageway in the sky, and the old bridge is available to pedestrians and local traffic. Iwade is a village which, ten years ago, probably held a couple of dozen houses. Now, ninety per cent of the fast expanding town is a sprawl of urban development. It is not entirely clear why anyone should want to live there but want it they certainly do.

The old bridge is quite good fun to walk across. On the other side, a path along the railway line would have represented a massive short cut to Queenborough. But notices warned not only that the land was private but that dogs would be shot; the implication was that humans were dispensable also. There might have been a footpath along the sea wall but it looked like a typical British footpath, meaning that it is very obscure and probably ends in a bog. I went on the huge loop to Queenborough instead.

Just at the outskirts of Queenborough, I stopped.

Why? Isn't this the fourth letter Q? Aren't you supposed to be researching the local culture, putting penetrating questions to the population, finding out whether there is a common denominator, establishing what it's like to live there?

This may be very unfair, but I wasn't sure whether there would be any culture at all in Queenborough. I will never know. It looked awful. I got to the outskirts and, by a bean field, decided that was enough. An estuary haze was settling over the landscape. It was forbidding, bleak and unpleasant. I had a train to catch. Furthermore, when I got back to Norfolk tonight I had a three-mile walk from the bus stop to home. I turned round and walked back to Sittingbourne.

Day 20: Sittingbourne to Maidstone
(17 July)

There has been a hiatus (or an hiatus?). Falling over on a tennis court, I banged and ricked my knee. For three weeks I have had no exercise. Could I start the walk again? I wrapped the knee in a bandage and took anti-inflammatories and painkillers and set off.

It was the hottest day of this or any other year. Britain was baking; today the temperature was well over thirty degrees. It was only twelve or thirteen miles to Maidstone but by the end I was well and truly pooped.

It is an extraordinary walk. Between the towns lies the ridge, stretching from Surrey to Dover, of the famous North Downs - known in theory to millions of school children and in practice to no-one. The ridge itself is narrow, sandwiched between two enormous motorways. Isolated farms, tracks, footpaths and homesteads crisscross around the top of the hills. Wildlife abounds. Huge views stretch across the Kent countryside. For an hour you are in a different world.

At right angles to my route runs the North Downs Way, a wondrous path through old world villages, past mansions and Pennine-type scenery. The best book on the route is written by the inimitable Kev Reynolds, who writes similar books about Switzerland. I have no idea who Kev is but he definitely writes my kind of guidebook. 'Walk forward for eighteen metres,' he will instruct, 'then turn left after the fourth oak tree. Mind the puddle!' This is exactly the help I need. Don't bother with the OS maps and compasses and altitude meters, give me firm and clear directions please.

Speaking of OS maps, I carried one today and tried to follow a big, hefty path from Sittingbourne, clearly marked as a byway. Needless to say, it was impenetrable; after battling against nettles, brambles and six-foot high grass I abandoned it in favour of the road. And what a road it became: the A249, dual carriageway, and very, very busy.

Near the top, a footbridge is called Jade's Crossing; it commemorates the little girl and her grandmother who were killed trying to cross the road before the bridge was built.

Then it was down to Maidstone, where the road passes round the back of the prison. I used to have numerous clients in there. The saddest was a man who was murdered while out for the afternoon. I carried on to the railway station in the heat.

Day 21: Maidstone to Yalding
(30 July)

I'm reading a novel by Barbara Kingsolver, a novel by Allan Gurganus and a novel by Herta Muller; a walking book by Terry Cudbird; *Edith and I* by Elizabeth Gowing; a book about

Egypt by Trevor Mostyn; and a memoir by Bob Marshall Andrews. I can't seem to finish any of them. After a train journey the current one always has about twenty pages left but then I pick up the next one. I'm way behind my schedule of fifty books in the year.

Somehow I came to Kent without a decent waterproof. Or footwear. And I forgot my knee bandage, painkillers and anti-inflammatories. All day the drizzle fell, sometimes harder, sometimes softer. Out of Maidstone ran the Medway Valley Walk. I didn't know this existed. As far as one could see through the veil of rain, this is a very lovely walk through empty woodlands. At one stage it left the river and rose into farmland with a manor on top; the views over Kent displayed the finest scenery so far.

The idea was to reach at least Queen Street - next of the Qs - today. Unfortunately, however, I went into Yalding station to check timetables; and at exactly that moment a cosy, comfortable, inviting train arrived at the platform. It beckoned me on a branch line to Paddock Wood and, irresponsibly and reprehensibly, I took it.

Q

On another subject, they want me to have a brain scan: presumably to see if I've got one. In fact they want to give me two brain scans, perhaps to see if I've got two brains. I'm also on the list for the cardiologist, the skin clinic, the throat clinic, the neurologist (again) and probably a few more that I can't remember. The joys of getting old. Revered for your wisdom, indulged with patience and understanding, never ignored, always asked for advice, always listened to about the old days...

In addition to the above, I've got ringworm.

Day 22: Yalding to QUEEN STREET to Paddock Wood
(9 September)

My friend Hugh said I should only walk to places beginning with Q when there is an R in the month. This is my excuse - along with all the other excuses - for not walking at all in August. I shall now walk between September and April. If I get off my arse.

It was only five or six miles and my knee hurt. I have booked a physio appointment. But at least we got to QUEEN STREET! Number five. Quidenham, Queen Adelaide, Quendon, Queenborough, Queen Street. Next, according to my calculations, I have to cross London and Surrey to get to Hampshire. Let's hope the sun hasn't set too many times.

After all this, I couldn't even find Queen Street. Standing helplessly at a junction, I was helped by a kind man with a van. Where was Queen Street? Just there, he said. I looked down. Ah! A street sign said - yes - Queen Street! It doesn't really seem to be a place as defined by the map; not surprisingly, perhaps, it is more like a street. There isn't any road sign marking the village and it's hard to know when you're in the village and when you're not. One can only assume that when you're somewhere else, you are no longer in Queen Street.

Finally I have spoken to someone in a place beginning with Q. Was he querulous? Quadrangular? What was it like living in Queen Street? Was it qualitative? Was it queer?

I forgot to ask.

For Paddock Wood, the man said, turn right at The Elm Tree. I did. In a while, the road twisting and turning, there it was: Paddock Wood station. I went home again. Must do better. Or find better excuses.

Day 23: Paddock Wood to Tonbridge
(20 September)

On the train going down to Tonbridge I had a nasty experience: a cup of Starbucks coffee. Like all right thinking people I have boycotted Starbucks since it emerged that they, like Amazon, think taxation doesn't apply to them. Now it seems they have acquired the concession for refreshments on the train line. I bought a coffee before I realised. It was revolting.

I'm worried about my annual reading schedule, which prescribes fifty books every year. Having just had a count up, I appear to be seriously in arrears for the first time in many years. The twin problems have been ridiculously long books and ridiculously bad writing. I have just finished a Kingsolver that wasn't nearly as good as usual. Yesterday I finished a book about Walthamstow that was crap. Today it was one by a Nobel Prize winner that was decidedly iffy. But at least they are all out of the way.

From Paddock Wood to Tonbridge runs a very straight railway line but no obvious road, so I found the way back to the Medway Valley Way. This ran through pleasant country into the heart of Tonbridge and I only got lost a few times. But after only three hours walking I was totally pooped. What's the matter with me? Have I just become unfit because of the knee injury? Perhaps Jennie the physio will sort me out.

Tonbridge appears to be a traditional English market town: charity shops, estate agents and pound shops. I ate an enormous bun which they now like to call a muffin or cupcake or some such Americanism. It's a bun.

Yesterday I was in Manchester and found myself giving out leaflets outside Minshull Street Crown Court. The very successful Probation Service is being carved up by the Tories so they can give presents to their shady friends who give money to the Conservative Party. What a corrupt government this is. Does anyone care?

Day 24: Tonbridge to Hildenborough
(3 October)

Oops! Things are not going very smoothly here.

I finished a bit of work in London at lunchtime and toddled down to Kent for a spot of walking. I was making my way through the labyrinth that is London Bridge station when - zip, bang - my heart went wrong.

This is only the third time in three and a half years, since the last procedure, that it has gone phut. On the other occasions it corrected itself. What would it do this time?

And, meanwhile, let's get this straight.

The bad knee is still there. Physio appointment tomorrow in the village with Jennie Tasker. Cardiology appointment on the 22nd. Next appointment with the neurologist on 3 November. Dermatology appointment on 8 October.

Waiting for an appointment with the throat person.

Anyone else I might have forgotten?

You're a bloody old wreck.

From London Bridge I got on the train to Tonbridge, hoping the heart would right itself. It didn't; it was all over the place. There didn't seem any point in going home again so I walked very, very slowly for ninety minutes in the rain to Hildenborough station. At this rate the whole trip will take thirty years.

Tonbridge has a castle. It also has a big private school; one wonders if the boys there have any idea how privileged they are. The Oast House Theatre was putting on a play by Terence Rattigan; it has probably been on since 1952. I came back to London and took another pill. At the time of writing, the heart is quiescent.

It's panic stations on the books. To meet my annual target I have to read eighteen books in thirteen weeks. Yesterday I knocked off a book by Trevor Mostyn which needed finishing. On the train I have been reading an Anita Shreve. On another train I read Alison MacLeod's *Unexploded*. Mustn't forget to enjoy them although that's not the most important factor.

Day 25: Hildenborough to Sevenoaks to Dunton Green
(9 October)

I had a very educational lunch....

But first, I exceeded my target for the day. As it happens, I was discussing targets at the weekend with friends Simon and Sally, since Simon is currently facing an appraisal. (On a farm. As he says, how does he factor the weather into his targets?)

I recommended my approach in my past professional life, which was to make sure that all targets were inevitably achieved without any effort and without any chance of failure. I found that 'Try to maintain my present standards' was very useful. As long as I tried... 'Think about referring clients to the hostel' was always a winner too. I thought very hard about it and thus met my target. The problem with targets is that as soon as you set them, someone tries to fiddle them. Or you get marked down for not achieving the unachievable. So keep them unmissable instead.

The target for the day was Sevenoaks. However, I reached it in under two hours. It had seemed likely that the only way on foot was off to the right through Knole Park, but it transpired that the main road had a footpath all along it. I needed no second invitation. Over the hill, down the dale and there it was.

Another private school straddled the entrance to town. They probably have major bloodbaths in sporting fixtures with Tonbridge. They also have the ugliest Leylandii hedge in town. Beyond the school stands the stately home of Knole, now owned by the National Trust and occupied by Lord Sackville or someone. I was to learn a lot about Knole and much, much more about life over lunch.

The bus station café was crowded and John invited me to share his table. He apologised for drinking coffee out of the saucer, which he said his grandson told him off for. Then he told me about his service in the Air Force during the Korean War. From there we discussed Americans, General MacArthur, carpet bombing ('pattern bombing'), the atom bomb, Stuffy

Dowding, Bomber Harris, Churchill, Chamberlain, Halifax and all the things chaps talk about when they get together. Unfortunately he could hear very little that I said, but his contribution was a lot more interesting than mine anyway. He had an encyclopaedic knowledge of Knole, knew all the history of Sevenoaks since the fifteenth century and, among other things, told me I must look at the oldest cricket ground in the county, The Vine, just up the road. So I did.

The next station up the line, Dunton Green, was not very far but the following one was too much for the day so I ambled up to Dunton Green and came away.

Oh, and I've got skin cancer.

That's being melodramatic. Yesterday I had an appointment at King's Lynn hospital for examination of a couple of spots on my face. Yes, they call them skin cancer but there's probably nothing to worry about. In a month they'll cut them out, give me a skin graft, pat me on the back and tell me to carry on.

Day 26: Dunton Green to Orpington
(14 October)

The aim of the day was to get back home in Norfolk in time for *University Challenge* at eight o'clock.

I didn't start out at Dunton Green until one.

Orpington lay the other side of the North Downs. This is really an extraordinary piece of geography. Hedged by motorways on all sides, close to London, very narrow, this slice of the North Downs does represent a wild country between thumping metropolises. The Downs are not very high but could be five thousand feet up.

Across the motorway the road led up to Knockholt, where it appears that some very affluent people live. Down again to Orpington, where I bought an egg mayo sandwich in Waitrose that was still frozen. I should have iced my swollen knee with it but I ate it, ice and all.

Pitched against a further walk in the semi-dark, the attraction of *University Challenge* unfortunately prevailed. Snobbishly, I like to say that I watch television on Monday for *University Challenge* and Saturday for *Match of the Day* and never in between the two. It's not quite true but it sounds good. The two programmes elicit the same response. 'I could have scored that goal!' 'I could have answered that!' Both are absolutely true. The trouble is that I couldn't have got into either team in the first place.

I reached home at 7.40 and just had time to re-heat the curry before 20.00.

Day 27: Orpington to Eltham
(20 October)

I am writing this up next day. As I write, Radio Norfolk has been playing the music of 1965 and 1974. Oh, happy days! They have played the Beatles, the Stones, Dylan, Manfred Mann, the Byrds and, glory be, the Animals. 'It's My Life and I'll Do What I Want!' Yes! It was the theme of the sixties.

The year 1974 produced curiosities. The station played music by Andy Fairweather Lowe. Well, Andrew Lowe, as he was in real life, played tennis for the South Wales over-35 team a few years later against Norfolk, and a very decent player he was too. In fact, I think the bastard beat me.

Finally Radio Norfolk played a song by Ken Boothe, 'Everything I Own'. Much later than 1974 I heard him sing this in concert in Kingston, Jamaica. On the same bill was the one and only Gregory Isaacs. If I have done nothing else with my life, I have heard Gregory Isaacs sing 'Night Nurse' in Kingston, Jamaica.

Back to the walking.

The best hours of the day, according to the weather forecast, would be from three to five in the afternoon. They would be dry. They would be arid. Orpington would be like the Gobi Desert.

True to form, at precisely three o'clock the thunder rolled and the rain splattered. I sheltered in Chislehurst railway station. I really, really, really, hate thunder.

The shortest route to central London seemed to lie through Petts Wood. Here began the London A-Z. Civilisation!

Orpington, Kent, is really Orpington, London, and from here the only break lies in the parks. I managed to get lost in Jubilee Park, quite an achievement. Then came Chislehurst Common, where the rich people live, and Chislehurst proper which is a good deal poorer. Over the brow of the hill the city of London displayed itself, resplendent. To one side, in the City itself, the Gherkin building stood guard. On the other side lay Canary Wharf, zooming into the sky, still a number of miles away but looking close enough to touch.

Eltham Palace is said to be very impressive but it was hidden from the road. It was acceptable to miss it; you can only take so much excitement in one day.

Day 28: Eltham to Limehouse
(25 October)

A day of great affluence (not mine) and dire poverty.

Nothing special happened in Eltham. Up the road to Shooter's Hill then along the A2 (busy) towards London. I haven't walked along here since heading in the opposite direction towards Venice several years ago. Suddenly the tedium of suburbia is broken by the huge grass expanse of Greenwich Park. I turned right, through the autumnal horse chestnut trees, to the Royal Observatory. The stupendous view stretches towards the National Maritime Museum and across the river to Canary Wharf. It's worth coming to London for.

Under the river, beside the *Cutty Sark*, the pedestrian tunnel leads to the north bank. It's very hard not to be looking up for leaks all the time while walking through the tunnel. I escaped to the other side where, on Mudchute DLR station, I was joined once again by my Companion. Needless to say, she had missed out all the boring bits and re-surfaced for the glamour.

We wandered down to Mudchute Farm, the large and lovely area under the lea of Canary Wharf where I used to take children to feed the animals: chickens, pigs, sheep, cattle and all the rest. Then we ventured into Canary Wharf itself.

It is just extraordinary. Like something from the future, the massive agglomeration of sky-piercing buildings, interspersed with walkways and the old docks, is totally cut off in every way from the rest of the world. Once, this was the Isle of Dogs, where gentle folk never ventured and which the rest of London only mentioned in hushed whispers. The lower half is Millwall, which speaks for itself.

(Sorry, Millwall. I once stood among the Millwall supporters at the old football ground, Cold Blow Lane, very silently supporting Norwich City. It was terrifying. I have a friend called Terry, the leading tattoo artist in Walthamstow, who is a famous Millwall supporter. He's pretty terrifying too but fortunately he's on my side. He is not on the side of anyone trying to sell drugs or otherwise misbehave near his studio. That's putting it politely. They don't do it twice.)

The Limehouse Cut (Canal) connects obscurely with the rest of the country. You can walk continuously along canals from here to Barnoldswick in Lancashire, where my friends Hugh and Val live. To do so is to reconnect with life. (There's a pretentious statement to finish the day with.)

Day 29: Limehouse to Vauxhall
(27 October)

This was just a couple of hours while I happened to pass through London. It's an interesting week. Monday in Kidderminster. Tuesday: Limehouse to Vauxhall. Wednesday: Bedfordshire to see Howard and Fiona. Thursday: Lewes in Sussex. Friday: take Mimi to Sheffield. Saturday: a visit to Reepham tennis club and then a trip to Norwich to visit not one but two old gits who have had knee replacements. So two hours today was all I could fit in. Well, that's what I told myself. Idleness played a part.

It began historically with a walk down Cable Street, scene of the Battle of Cable Street in 1936. The fascist movement, led by Oswald Mosley, marched in the East End. The working class, Jewish and non-Jewish, rose up and smashed them. Ever since, the various fascist movements in Britain have never thrived.

From here, the road led over splendid Tower Bridge and along the even more splendid South Bank, all the way past Southwark Cathedral, the Golden Hind, the Globe Theatre, the Tate Modern, the Festival Hall complex (hideous unfortunately) and the Wheel. The whole area has been transformed into a cornucopia of tourist attractions. Views across the river to the City of London, St Paul's and the Houses of Parliament are simply staggering. Across Europe it is half term this week, and most of Europe's children are here. We (Companion and I) finished the day at Vauxhall, which is certainly not a tourist attraction. I went to do the bar at my tennis club in Wanstead, where we discussed the Battle of Cable Street.

Day 30: Vauxhall to Clapham Junction (rain stopped play)
(9 November)

First, the worst news of the week. Last night on the tube a young woman insisted on giving up her seat for me. I protested but to no avail. Oh dear. Do I look that old?

The nadir will be reached when pregnant women give me their seat.

Second worst news. The hospital says I have definitely got Parkinson's Disease.

Well, that's really not very good.

Anyway, I was in London to watch the tennis at the O2 yesterday and had to catch the 2.30 from Liverpool Street to Norwich today for the football (5.30 kickoff). Rain was forecast for one o'clock so it seemed a good idea to snatch a couple of hours first from Vauxhall and head out of London.

As I stepped out of Vauxhall tube station at 10.30 the rain started.

By 10.32 it was raining doorknobs.

I wasn't equipped; this was supposed to be a casual stroll through London. Within the hour I was soaked.

Past Battersea Power Station, the ugliest building in London, huge and hideous. Why they want to develop it I can't imagine. Past Battersea Dogs' Home. Endless 364 buses to Liverpool Street went past and I resisted them. Eventually I gave in. The bus was likely to be warmer and would certainly be drier. Pathetic.

But we won the football.

Day 31: Clapham Junction to Richmond
(12 November)

Yesterday I was in a prison, talking to some inmates about books. As part of the process we asked everyone to write a short piece beginning: 'I walked out of the door and down the stairs.'

One of the inmates was a young lad, no more than twenty-one. All the other men contributed something worthwhile on the required subject but he ignored it and wrote what he wanted. He wrote about getting up in the morning, at home, and having a bath. That's all, just having a bath. I don't know how long he had been inside but what he dearly wanted was just to be at home, being normal, just having a bath. When he wanted to.

Normally I come to Clapham Junction for meetings at my trade union's head office. This time I walked back from the station to where I left off last time and turned left. A lovely walk runs from here along the river. I didn't take that. Instead I followed my nose, having forgotten to bring my A-Z, and the nose led into Wandsworth, then Putney Bridge, Putney Common and Barnes Common to Mortlake. That's where they run the Boat Race, Putney to Mortlake, or is it Mortlake to Putney? From here all roads led to Richmond.

First, though, Carol's Place in East Sheen turned out to be the best café for many a mile. Carol seems to open when she feels like it, and the establishment dispenses wisdom as much as its excellent food. Two customers were debating the utility and mobile phone companies. 'They're all capitalists. And capitalism is immoral anyway.' Yes! Then Carol herself intervened. 'He's got a lot to answer for, that Tim Berners-Lee.' (Poor Berners-Lee, the greatest philanthropist in history when he gave away the internet.) 'What one man invents, another man will abuse.' Well, that's true.

A seventy-five-year-old working in the café showed me how straight his back was. His sons are the same apparently; it's in the genes.

I left full of good will and finished the day at Richmond station.

Day 32: Richmond to Hampton Court
(27 November)

The other day I was watching tennis in Tipton, West Midlands, which must be one of the most deprived areas of the country. The contrast with Richmond, well....

Tipton has no shops, not even charity shops; no-one gives clothes away. Richmond town centre is bustling with shoppers, including me; I bought some underwear in M&S. Richmond has splendid buildings leading down to the beautiful river and opulent houses on the river bank. It has wildlife: a heron landed about five yards from me and the famous south-west London parakeets are everywhere. In the park the deer are rutting at this time of year; stags clash their antlers feverishly and everyone, motorised or pedestrian, has to give way to them. Tipton has none of these things, nor ever will have.

Down the road a couple of miles is Latchmere House, always a favourite prison to visit. A pleasant walk through Ham led to the prison, a successful institution where all the inmates went out daily to work. Wormwood Scrubs it wasn't.

Since my last day's walking I have had a couple of bits dug out of my face at King's Lynn hospital. The surgeon did a super job and now you can hardly see the scars. We wait to see the analysis of the bits.

At Kingston Bridge my sister Susan joined me for the afternoon section. This inevitably meant that little progress would be made. She took me across the park to Hampton Court, built by Henry VIII and pretty spectacular too. By the time we had had a cup of tea and the excessive talking that went with it, darkness was falling and I caught the train home.

Last week Susan and Wally and I and Sarah and Ben and my Companion and a load of Susan's friends went to the Thursford Christmas Spectacular, the best night out of the year, a wildly over the top music and dance package, with a hundred and thirty professional performers, in the middle of nowhere in Norfolk. Two shows per day for six weeks and the punters come in busloads from all over the country. Personally I can't wait for next year.

Day 33: Hampton Court to Walton-on-Thames
(4 December)

This week it was constipation.

There really is nothing worse than constipation - nothing so far at any rate. It happened to me once before when I was taken off warfarin too suddenly. This time I was put on Parkinson's medication suddenly. For glamour, constipation ranks alongside an ingrowing toenail: a painful problem which brings nothing but humiliation and which everyone else finds very funny.

Once in Boulder, Colorado, I had an infected ingrowing toenail. I managed to find the poor people's (free) hospital, where they took a look, gave me an injection and then sliced me open without waiting for it to work. Finally they packed me off in agony on to the streets of Boulder; the treatment didn't work and I eventually got sorted out in New Zealand. For years afterwards they pursued me for money for the ineffective drugs they had given me. After a couple of years I gave in and sent the money, with a little homily pointing out that capitalism's medicine had failed me but that New Zealand's socialist system had succeeded. I'm sure they cared.

Tonight we were catching a plane from Heathrow to Switzerland; I very strongly disapprove of flying when there is an alternative but I didn't make the decision. Heathrow is very close to Hampton Court so I came down early from Norfolk to pack in an hour's walking first. Hampton Court to Sunbury, cross the river and catch the bus to the airport. The flight was at seven o'clock and I should be there comfortably by four.

Only one problem with this plan: no bridge at Sunbury. I had misread the map.

I walked on to Walton, not far. By all accounts a bus from there should take no more than forty minutes and I should reach Heathrow by five, still in comfortable time.

The first bus didn't come at all.

The next one was of course crammed full. Then it was delayed: Friday night brought the busiest traffic of the week. We drove round, apparently in circles, for an hour. Where were we? Oh, Sunbury, after an hour. Apparently it might 'possibly' take another forty-five minutes to Heathrow. Arrival at 6.15?

Then because the bus was now thirty minutes late they made us get off it and on to another one which would be even later.

Finally a dispute broke out. Two young women refused to fold their buggies to enable a wheelchair user to get on board the bus. Wheelchair users have priority so they were told that if they refused to fold they would have to leave the bus. They refused this too. This one seemed unlikely to be resolved before Christmas, never mind my departure time, so I got off the bus. Opposite was a supermarket; I could get a taxi from there because you could always get a taxi from a supermarket.

There was a ninety minute wait for a taxi. All the firms were the same. It was now 5.30. And the bus had left without me.

In the petrol station a black cab was filling up. I asked if he was free. No. He was off duty, on his way to visit his daughter in Camberley.

Plaintively, I said I had a plane to catch.

What time?

I told him.

'Give me a few minutes,' he said.

He went over and paid for the petrol, then came back. 'I'll take you,' he said.

Thank you thank you thank you.

Going straight there would take years. The only way was round the M25. I paid, of course, the normal meter rate, which was nearly as much as the flight to Switzerland. On the way we talked about Cuba, where he had a young child whom he visited six times per year. It was a very enjoyable journey.

I arrived at Terminal Five at 5.55 and I was met, of course, by withering sarcasm. Such is life.

Day 34: Nowhere to Nowhere
(24 December)

I bought a ticket to Walton-on-Thames. I travelled to Vauxhall to pick up the train there. I asked various station staff when the next train to Walton would stop by. The universal response was nothing but a dazed look. Eventually the man who knows came along (there always is one somewhere) and they referred the question to him.

He put his head on one side and shook it.

'Are you planning to come back again?' he enquired.

I indicated that I was.

He shook his head again.

'There's floods,' he said. 'There's trees down. There's speed restrictions. You've just missed a train. There might be another one in an hour. But coming back again...'

He was right. South-west London, the place where bad weather doesn't dare to go, has been flooded and blown to pieces. Weybridge, playground of the rich, is submerged. Gales and downpours have lashed southern Britain and the epicentre has been Weybridge, just beyond Walton-on-Thames. Global warming is invading in the form of terrible storms.

I turned round and went home.

My friend Margaret lives in Walton-on-Thames. I had contacted her to see if she would like to go walking today. Strangely, she seemed to have other things to do on 24 December.

Day 35: Walton-on-Thames to Woking
(29 December)

The Basingstoke Canal...

It doesn't sound as romantic as Venice. It sounds like something you're sentenced to: 'Five years penal servitude on the Basingstoke Canal...' It has been an intermediary target for a while and finally it arrived.

The Thames was coursing fast, still flooding, still rampaging and bubbling. Where the Wey joins it, a ferry carries the Thames Path walkers across the junction. Except that it doesn't: flooded off, no ferry. For those of us seeking the Basingstoke Canal, though, it was no problem. The path followed the Wey Navigation Channel for a few miles, then branched off again for the canal.

Weybridge, land of the rich. A few years ago the Norfolk over-something tennis team (fifty-five? sixty? Don't remember) played a match at the Weybridge club. This is situated within the most exclusive estate in the country, stuffed with the houses of pop stars and golfers. We were just country boys so we thought we'd have a little tour round after the match. We set off. Within two minutes we were being tailed, or escorted, by a surly big black motor. It stayed there until we left the estate.

My Companion came today and we saw something much more colourful than a pop star: a kingfisher. It was worth coming down here just for this.

Back home I have a Stephen Durrant photograph of a kingfisher over my mantelpiece. Stephen tried to get a kingfisher to perch on a bottle of Kingfisher lager but it wouldn't co-operate. Instead he put a full glass beside the bottle. The bird perched on the glass, almost pecking at the bottle, and Stephen got a spectacular photograph.

Extraordinary houseboats line the canal. They look like giant caravans merely transplanted to the waterside.

Woking is famous for its waste management. (Well, it's better than nothing.) I don't know anything else about Woking except the route to the tennis club.

They told me that the bits they dug out of my face aren't dangerous. Well, that's one life threatening condition I haven't got, anyway.

Day 36: Woking to Farnborough
(2 January)

My New Year's resolution is to read one book more than last year.

For the last fifty-seven years I have kept a list of all the Books I Have Read. Generally, in fact almost always, I have met my target of fifty books for the year when I add them up on 31 December. This year it was - disastrously - only forty-nine. I had to read four between Christmas and New Year and sank so low that I read a book of poetry. On 31 December I finished Andrew O'Hagan's novel about Marilyn Monroe's dog but I was still one short.

Now I'm reading Martha Gellhorn, always good value, given to me for Christmas by my friend Jane. It's a book about awful travel experiences; I'm so glad I don't do that sort of thing any more. I'm also reading a novel by Robert Wilton, whom I stayed with in Kosovo. Waiting after that is a book by Robert Macfarlane given to me by my friend Judy and, peculiarly, two books by people called John Williams. One of them is *Stoner*, given to me by Em and Dave, and the other is a Cardiff-based crime novel obtained from the post office book exchange in my village.

Martha Gellhorn includes a story about travelling in China in 1941. Apart from her companion, she hadn't seen a western face for some weeks and had been travelling in appalling conditions. Getting in to a town she suddenly spotted a Caucasian. She turned to her colleague:

'Bet you twenty Chinese dollars he's from St Louis.'

'Why?'

'I think it's a law. When you go to the worst, furthest place, the stranger has come from St Louis.'

'Done.'

She won twenty Chinese dollars, of course.

Q

Back in England, storms have been lashing down again. Yesterday there were floods. Tomorrow there will be floods. The Basingstoke Canal has water cascading in and water flowing out. Rivers have overflowed, many areas are deluged and thousands have had power cut off. Today's walking was an oasis. Rain fell only at the end.

This is a strange area. Pirbright army camp lines one side of the road. Beyond it lies Deepcut Barracks, scene of the terrible scandal surrounding the death of a young recruit. On the other side of the canal is a Danger Area; only railway lines and the canal cross it. The canal climbs steadily in an endless series of locks. There must be nice countryside around here; unfortunately I couldn't see any of it because the canal lies generally in a dip.

I managed to take a wrong turning, not an easy thing to do when following a canal, and found myself in Mytchett where a nice woman set me right.

Day 37: Farnborough to Hook
(10 January)

England is still submerged.

The south-east has been flooded for a week but now it is mostly the Thames area. Did the radio say it has got a hundred times its normal volume of water? Trains are cancelled and whole towns are submerged. Still it keeps raining. Today was a good day; rain fell only in the afternoon.

The Basingstoke Canal leads unsurprisingly to Basingstoke. However, it goes round half of England to get there and I abandoned it for the roads and the woods. Thanks to the good work of Hampshire County Council, moreover, footpaths abound.

Before Hampshire CC there was Brenda Parker. I don't know who Brenda is or was, but the world is indebted to her for the footpath named after her and leading to Fleet

Pond, a lake which allegedly has been there for an historical time. As the rain fell, I pushed on down country lanes, through Winchfield and over the M3. It was delightful to find footpaths all the way to Hook, although walking along the A30 might not have been everyone's idea of a fun afternoon.

I can't come back for a couple of weeks due to child care responsibilities. That is the pompous phrase that men use when they occasionally have charge of a child and feel they have to tell the world about it. Me too. Anyway, that's my excuse for leaving the walk for a while.

Day 38: Hook to Basingstoke
(2 February)

During the miners' strike of 1984-85 it was one's duty to go out every night to benefit gigs to raise money for the miners and their families. One night, an impressive northern miner made a speech describing their fund raising efforts. 'They told me to go to Basingstoke. I said: "where's Basingstoke?" They said it was in Hampshire. I said: "where's Hampshire?"' He was sure they were wasting their time; no-one in the south of England would give money to the miners. When they got there they were overwhelmed by their reception and by the hospitality; the south of England welcomed them with open arms and donated hand over fist. It wasn't only the north that hated Thatcher and everything she stood for.

For a few hours it stopped raining. This is getting tedious; the Met Office has said that the whole of southern England could be flooded and Somerset already is. Grabbing this window of opportunity I popped down to Hants and walked for little more than a couple of hours. It was straight down the A30. There is nothing worth saying about it.

Basingstoke town centre is reminiscent of Rotterdam; a collection of the world's ugliest new buildings appears to have been dropped at random from the sky. They don't even have the excuse that it was bombed to pieces in the war. Perhaps it should be.

I'm reading a very pretentious book about walking that I was given for Christmas. It is very, very pretentious. It's a shame really because he writes well when he's not trying to be so bloody clever; but he's got sixty-eight pages of notes including thirteen pages of bibliography. On every page is a literary allusion. Listen, mate, I want to say to him. It's just a bloody book. We really don't care if you've read Kierkegaard.

At the same time I'm reading the two books by John Williams; or rather two books by two John Williamses. It's like the time when the two John Williamses, JPR and JJ, played rugby for Wales at the same time; perhaps these two authors should be known by their initials. (Incidentally I lost twice to JPR at tennis.) One John Williams wrote *Stoner*, republished this year and a massive literary success, beautifully written and immensely depressing. The other John Williams writes about crime in Cardiff.

My friend Jon in Derby has a sent me a page from Bartholomew's *Gazetteer of the British Isles*, 1965 edition. Only Jon would have such a document in his possession. It has a list of places beginning with Q. I can't understand it all and I won't be going to parishes beginning with Q or localities or islands. I now know, however, that Quidenham had a population of ninety-eight in 1965. It had 1,142 acres too. Queen Adelaide's population was apparently not worthy of mention but Quendon had 124 inhabitants. Queenborough was a whopper at 2,941 and ran ferries to Flushing, while Queen Street was only a hamlet but had a post office. Wasn't that useful?

Day 39: Basingstoke to Overton
(5 February)

My Companion (who has not come today or at any time this winter) announced that it would be 'wimpish' not to go walking today. The south of England is ravaged still by flood, gales and general pestilence. Somerset is under water - and ferocious gales were forecast for today. The railway line through Devon has been ripped apart and Cornwall is cut off. Trains west of

Salisbury are delayed or cancelled. But it would be wimpish not to go walking out of Basingstoke.

Prince Charles has donned his gumboots and gone to Somerset. He has said all the right things, stopping just short of calling the government incompetent, uncaring fools (who had cut all expenditure so much that there is no flood protection). It is reminiscent of Edward VIII, when Prince of Wales, visiting the impoverished Welsh valleys and proclaiming, 'Something must be done. Something will be done.' They ought to make Charles the Minister for Floods. When they made Denis Howell Minister for Drought in 1976 the rains came immediately and the problem ended.

Yes: a vicious, blustery, heaving gale was howling round my lugholes when I set out from Basingstoke. After an hour or so, contrary to the forecast, it mellowed down to just a good solid rain. It couldn't be called a pleasant afternoon. Most of it was spent hopping on to the bank because the road had no footpath. Overton arrived in the end. That's about all there is to say.

Earlier a couple of cedars stood in the middle of a ploughed field. This must be unprecedented. The hall beyond, now a hotel, must once have had parkland where the cedar trees stood. When they were planted, two or three hundred years ago, no-one envisaged a future where ancient estates fell on hard times, the manor house was sold and the parkland was ploughed up for agriculture.

Overton is next door to - yes - Quidhampton (Hants)! At last another Q. What would it be like? So far there is no sign. Indeed there is no signpost. This must be why no-one walks round the Qs. I am half a mile from Quidhampton and there is no signpost to it, just as there was no sign for Queen Street in Kent. Is this a conspiracy? Are they keeping the Qs secret?

The Gallery tea room supplied a cream scone, then I took the bus back to Basingstoke. I do love a bus full of noisy school children. These eleven-year-olds were full of the joys of life and very, very silly. Then two teenage girls, about fourteen, sitting behind me talked about crushes they used to have on boys when they were young and silly. (The boys were all called Jack or Ben.) It was good fun.

Day 40: Overton to QUIDHAMPTON
to Andover
(10 February)

Because of the Parkinson's, my voice has grown faint and I have been referred to the speech therapist, Karen. She has given me exercises and has suggested that I practise regular phrases that I use in life and in work. What, she asked, were common phrases that I used in this trade union work that I did? What did I say most often?

I thought about it.

"'That's not acceptable,'" I said.

'Ok,' Karen said, 'that's fine. What else do you say often, perhaps when you're travelling about?'

"'A return to Dartford please!" And "No sugar!'"

Which was how I came to be along the B3400 through the woods, proclaiming 'That's not acceptable!' at the top of my voice. Then 'A return to Dartford please! No sugar!' I did feel a bit of a prat: the mad man on the bus, the one you don't want to sit next to, suddenly shouting out 'That's not acceptable!' at full volume.

Quidhampton. Here we are now. Are we? There was indeed no sign. There was Quidhampton Farm and Quidhampton Business Units but there appeared to be nothing identifying Quidhampton itself. Is it to confuse the invading enemy, to throw them into total disorientation because they can't find Quidhampton?

Two men walking prams, two men walking dogs and one runner passed by; but I chickened out of asking any of them. However, reliable information has it that the word 'quid' (for a pound) derives from here because the De La Rue paper mill, which prints bank notes, lies just up the hill.

Other reliable information stated that Whitchurch would receive a shower of rain at one o'clock but that otherwise the day would be clear. Well, Whitchurch did have a shower of rain at two o'clock and Andover had one at three o'clock. Fair enough. But Whitchurch also had a bloody great lacerating hail storm at eleven o'clock, so sudden that I couldn't even get the waterproofs on. Was this their shower of rain?

H's Coffee Shop in Whitchurch kindly provided Marmite on toast, enough to keep the tourists going through the afternoon. People are visiting the local silk mill or walking in the pleasant countryside; or, at least, they would be if it wasn't totally submerged. Footpaths abound but are all going in the wrong direction even if they are visible and not waterlogged. I pressed along the roads to Andover, which seems a nice old market town. I didn't stop.

The route passed the Watership Down Inn. Was it written here?

Day 41: Andover to QUARLEY to Grateley
(1 March)

I almost forgot about Quarley. Plotting a quick route to Salisbury based on the main A30 road, the next letter Q almost passed by unnoticed. Fortunately I spotted it at the last minute and set off into the sunshine.

Yes, sunshine. March is different. Anyone who remembers the big freeze of 1962-63 will know that sunshine has a different timbre to it in March. Snow melts, new snow doesn't settle and reasonable life begins again. This year it is so warm that daffodils are out in balmy Hampshire alongside crocuses, primroses and cherry blossom. Somerset is still under water but everywhere else is just warm and wet.

It is a year now since I started this walk in the freezing cold. At the outset I intended to do a huge chunk in a couple of months. Hah. More realistically I hoped to do it all in a couple of years. Now it doesn't seem likely. I have been away since I last walked and I'm going away again for a fortnight. Perhaps I'll crack on when I get back...

Out of Andover, the road passed a large army base and an even larger Co-op warehouse. The roads grew smaller, the fields larger. Monxton is a village with more thatched houses than I have ever seen. Is it famous? To the right, an imposing manor house loomed over the countryside. Was that a water garden or was it just flooded?

Beside the road a sign advertised RON BAILLIE AND APES. Whatever could it mean? A few yards further stood another sign. KIERON BAILLIE LANDSCAPE SERVICES. Someone had borrowed some of the letters.

I asked a man in green trousers what was happening in Quarley. 'Very little,' he said. However, he added it had one interesting feature. Until recently the church bells stood at ground level, not up in the tower. Unfortunately they were no more. Taking advantage of their accessibility, someone stole two of them.

Again Quarley was a village without a road sign. Nothing told me I was entering Quarley. It becomes curiouser and curiouser, this obliteration of all things Q.

A few months ago I caught a train in Grateley after a bit of work in HMP Erlestoke; the prison librarian dropped me off at the station on her way home. Now I caught another train. Back in April, I suppose.

Day 42: Grateley to Salisbury
(9 April)

Yes, April. Holidays, work and idleness intervened. Now spring is here, cool and clear. Everything is early: the blackthorn is in blossom, the oilseed rape is in flower and the corn is growing. It looks like mid-May.

Along the railway line from Grateley a bridleway led into a country idyll, not a building in sight. It looked promising but it didn't last the hour. To the right, a massive air force base emerged: fighters, transport plane and helicopters zoomed around the countryside, spoiling everyone's morning. Even worse lay to the left. Across the railway line all kinds of nasties prohibited public access. This is Porton. Is this the home of chemical weapons? Whatever it is, it made the rape fields grow but I don't want any.

The bridleway petered out at a football field as they do. Various Winterbourne villages came and went. (Place name of the day: Winterbourne Dauntsey. Where do they get them from?) Through highways and byways Salisbury arrived.

What a place! From many miles away the famous cathedral was a landmark. The town centre is old and big. The town square is memorable. Tourists thronged. Nice town. Sorry, city.

That was Salisbury.

Day 43: Salisbury to QUIDHAMPTON (2) to Tisbury
(have lost the date before typing this up; but some time in April)

We went for a walk, my Companion and I, around lovely Salisbury. All the previous accolades still apply. It was cosy and ancient.

It is hard to find anything to say about Quidhampton number 2, just outside Salisbury. It's there and it's another one ticked off the list. That was it. We turned away, chased by a million motorbikes (it's Sunday), past Wilton Hall and up to the bridleway by the racecourse.

This was another bridleway that must have gone somewhere at some time. Perhaps it led to some old earthworks which I ought to know more about. Steadily but inexorably it led up a gentle incline, shrouded by trees and hedges and fields. It was idyllic but tedious, like walking along canals. Then, quite suddenly, we came out at those earthworks, high up, gazing over many miles of countryside. On the other side of the big mound are images made of white stones, like the white horses famously dotted around. These images, though, are of badges. How peculiar. Badges of what? Regiments? They may be.

Descending steeply, we got involved with a sheep farming family who needed more hands to block off the road and herd the sheep. The sheep pretended, as sheep do, to be traumatised by the whole event. When they saw their new pasture, however, deep and lush and green, they managed to overcome their trauma. Very soon, silence reigned apart from chewing noises; bleating ceased. Recently I asked my sister Sarah how her surviving chickens were coping after a fox attack. She said that twenty-four hours later they were fine. 'Chickens have short memories.' So have sheep.

After another bridleway we took to footpaths and inevitably got lost, but eventually we reached Tisbury.

Back home, the GP has done a memory test. She said it was useful to spot early signs of dementia in Parkinson's. Cheery. It had nothing to do with getting lost on footpaths though.

Day 44: Tisbury to QUEEN OAK (?) to Gillingham (Dorset)
(21 April)

Why is Gillingham (Dorset) pronounced with a hard G but Gillingham (Kent) with a soft one?

I had nearly forgotten Queen Oak. At the start I was just about to set off on a straight line from Tisbury to Gillingham when I noticed a little circle on the map. Ah yes, Queen Oak. Oh dear, I've got to go up there.

By the end of the day I wished I had never heard of it.

But there were other problems. This week it's the back. I made the mistake of digging a trench to plant the potatoes. On the same day a fight broke out in the train I was on. No, there was no connection with the potatoes, but moving rather swiftly to avoid the fight I stretched down and away to grab my bag and leave the carriage. Yaah! A stabbing pain. In the orthopaedic section my knee has recently been ok; in fact the bad knee has been better than the good knee (or vice versa). Now the back can take over instead.

You would think that of all the pills I take, one of them would sort it out. But the pills just make me feel sick. In general, I don't know whether I feel grim because of the pills, because I'm knackered or just because I'm grim.

Between Tisbury and Hindon lie affluent houses, rolling hills and generally very pleasant countryside. However, half of England was driving down the lane between the two. Where are they all going? Well, it's Easter Monday and they're all celebrating the Resurrection (again) in the garden of the pub. Then doing it again in another pub. They were very joyful.

The route off the roads emerged at Hindon in the form of the Monarch's Way, where trampled Charles II on his escape from the Battle of Worcester in 1651 (so the sign says). Robert Wilton wrote about it in his excellent novel. (Yes, he's my friend but it's true.) The king wouldn't get far nowadays. Within a month it will be overgrown completely, a typical English footpath. Eventually it cleared but by then I was stuffed and took to the lanes and then an easy footpath into Mere.

En route, the bridleway suddenly entered a clearing right at the top of a hill. I had no idea it had climbed so far. On all sides, three hundred and sixty degrees, massive views lay over lower ground and other ridges. At least three counties lay below.

No-one in Mere had ever heard of Queen Oak. For that matter, I don't think anyone in Queen Oak had ever heard of Queen Oak. I don't think it exists.

The young woman in the Co-op, however, gave good advice on walking to Bourton by a route which, according to the map, ought to go through Queen Oak. It certainly went through Zeals, which appeared to contain a stately home. Why aren't I walking round the Zs? There are only five of them. From Zeals I carried on to Bourton. Where was Queen Oak? Was it down that little cul-de-sac, the only road to the left? Is it a place or is it just an Oak? Where the bloody hell?

Gillingham was a long, long way away and seemed rather nondescript (sorry, Gillingham); but bevies of people gave very helpful directions so that made up for it. Darkness fell before I arrived.

One of the problems with walking along byways is that I find it impossible not to start singing Frank Sinatra's 'My Way'. Oh no!

Day 45: Er, Sherborne to Templecombe
(22 April)

Sometimes I cheat.

I had no intention of cheating on this trip; all that was behind me. However, after yesterday's walk I could hardly get out of bed this morning and something had to give.

Cheating is doing the walk backwards. No, I don't mean actually walking backwards, silly. I mean that instead of walking from Gillingham to Sherborne I would walk from Sherborne to Gillingham. The same route but in reverse.

I stayed the night in Sherborne and should have taken the train to Gillingham, walked back and then taken the same train again. Stuff that. I set out to walk very slowly to Gillingham. I managed the very slowly bit but only made it as far as Templecombe, less than halfway.

But what an extraordinary place is Milborne Wick. It came straight out of *Lark Rise to Candleford*, a totally preserved version of English countryside, circa 1878. The village must be besieged by film location managers. In addition to the houses and the stream and the old mill, it has

(a) bluebells, (b) ducks, (c) a water wheel. For a while I stood and gaped.

Another English tradition was not so welcome: the meaningless footpath that disappears instantly into a field, never to be seen again. Don't be fooled by a shiny new sign. Twice I fell for it and spent half an hour walking pointlessly in circles. Too bad tempered to continue, I took the train at Templecombe and will do the rest later.

Day 46: Sherborne to QUEEN CAMEL to Podimore
(8 May)

Sherborne is a remarkable place. It has two castles, which is plain greedy. It has two private schools. As far as I know one is for boys and one for girls. It has a monster of an abbey. Most of the town was built an awfully long time ago. In the abbey vestibule I listened to a couple of hundred adolescent boys belting out a hymn. What certainty, what absolute confidence they have in their place in the world of the future.

The scenic route out of Sherborne lay up through a lovely valley. Streams coursed down both sides from the top. Sandford Orcas lived up to its genteel name, full of large and exquisite stone houses. Where do the poor people live? Marston Magna (another name to savour) was all right too, but from there on the walking involved jumping into hedges on the main road. I tried a succession of footpaths but, true to form, they disappeared straight into fields of long wet grass with no exit. Then came Queen Camel.

The village has a shop but no pub; usually it's the reverse. I sat in the bus shelter to eat my sandwich and read the paper. So what is there to say about this latest letter Q? Well, the name has nothing to do with camels and the actual history is too boring to repeat. It's a busy little place on a main road and seems keen on pottery and planes. That's more or less it.

Yeovilton airfield seems to be a training centre for helicopters (or rather for their pilots). It also contains the Fleet Air Arm Museum, said to be the largest naval aviation museum in Europe. I have no doubt it is. I suspect it is also the smallest.

I think Bill Edrich was in the Fleet Air Arm during the war: the famous combative cricketer from Norfolk who with Denis Compton transformed the nation in 1947. In the war he was stationed in Norfolk and spent the mornings being shot at and the afternoons playing cricket. I played against Edrich once when he was middle aged (and combative). He had the biggest forearms I have ever seen except for Rod Laver's, whom I once stood beside in the queue for a cup of tea.

Playing in the same match was the legendary Michael Falcon, then aged seventy-five. Falcon captained Norfolk before the First World War and after the Second World War. Think about that.

Last night Norwich City were relegated from the Premier League. They managed this without even playing as other results consigned them to doom. It cast a pall over the day.

Day 47: Podimore to Ilchester to Yeovil (wrong direction)
(9 May)

I sneezed as I left Chilthorne Domer.

'Bless you!' came a consoling cry from somewhere. It was ethereal: above, below, all around. It turned out to be rather more mundane. It was a bloody cyclist.

It was an unusual expression of goodwill from the cycling fraternity, all of whom had morosely ignored my cheery greetings yesterday. Today, however, was different. Every pedestrian said hello. Even cyclists smiled. Only the walking was disastrous.

A couple of miles further was Ilchester. The plan was to take the bus to Yeovil then the train back to Templecombe, then walk to fill in the few miles I had missed. Instead I decided on the clever route for cheats. I would walk back to Yeovil, a similar distance, and count this as the miles missed.

No more cheating!

It began well with a stroll across the Ilchester Mead, a fine example of common land and permanent pasture. The Monarch's Way went clearly - on the map - in my direction.

Memo to the guardians of the Monarch's Way: it doesn't exist.

It's all very well putting up signs every couple of miles; there has got to be a path in between. This one just disappeared. I walked round three sides of a hay field and climbed creakily over some fences. A wet knee-high field of grass was next to be cut for hay. A deer and two yellowhammers were poised for something. It all took a very long time. Eventually a road emerged and Yeovil lay beyond, but that wasn't the end of it. I went to the wrong station.

Right on the other side of town, you could see the station on the map. A train left at 2.29. I belted along, dirty and weary, and reached the station at 2.28. I would grab a ticket and leap on the train.

It was very quiet.

On my map there was only one station. The other one, Yeovil Junction, was on the next map.

'That's a little disappointing,' I thought. Or something like that.

Extraordinarily, Pen Mill station had a buffet, kept by a man who had been there eighteen years. He got me a taxi. (The bus timetable said it would take fifteen minutes but the driver said it was forty by bus.) The taxi driver had just returned from a trip to South Mimms, a bit of an earner, and tomorrow he has a trip to Heathrow, a return home and then a trip to Gatwick. His longest ever run was to Newcastle. A man got off a coach at Yeovil at three in the morning having travelled from Spain. He didn't care if it cost £500 to Newcastle because he had just won £15,000 at the Casino. He pulled out the money and off they went.

Day 48: Yeovil to Ilminster
(1 June)

'You've got a temperature!' my Companion said accusingly.

'No I haven't.'

'You've got a temperature.'

Yes, dear. But I didn't actually say 'yes dear' since I value my life.

I had a map. She had modern technology and she was in charge, so we walked for an extra hour in a wide circle to follow the technological route. I was stoical. We walked eventually about seventeen miles.

A succession of hilly, stony villages housed bursting streams. Little Norton, Norton Hamdon, Over Stratton and Seavington St Michael, then down the main road to Ilminster. In the pub, a customer who had seen us on the main road seemed surprised that we were alive. Then Ilminster, a pleasant little town with a very unattractive church (minster?).

It's an awful long way to Queen Dart, the next letter Q. And Devon is an even longer way from real life.

Day 49: Ilminster to Taunton
(2 June)

On the train at the end of the day I embarked on a virtual impossibility for a man with my malady: change a very sweaty walking shirt for a rather tight normal shirt with buttons.

1. In the tiny toilet, try to pull sweaty shirt off by the neck.

2. Having failed, try from the waist.

3. Banging around the walls of the toilet, go back to the neck.

4. Stooping low from the waist, eventually tug it off.

5. Get clean shirt on one arm.

6. Stretch arm up to ceiling, normal technique for Parkinson's.

7. Fail to get rest of shirt on. One arm not really enough.

8. Bang round walls again.

9. Get shirt half on but realise have mismatched buttons against holes. Re-button.

10. Finally succeed. Twenty minutes after entering toilet, return to seat exhausted.

Today should have been a doddle, but British footpath signs and British road signs, not to mention British new technology (again), brought a frazzled, spitting and cursing five-hour stretch. We climbed fences, we followed tractor tracks instead of paths, we aimed for bridleways that never materialised, we never, of course, lost our tempers.

Why do they signpost Taunton as being one mile away when in reality it is three? Is it to encourage us? To take the piss out of us? To make us miss our train?

The cricket ground at Taunton is very close to the station. Maybe next time...

Days 50-51: Taunton to Wellington
to Tiverton Parkway
(3 and 4 July)

In the middle of a field was a young woman on a thousand-mile walk.

Ollie is a student at Leeds, doing cultural studies and Japanese. (Cultural studies, she explained, means philosophy and English.) She is spending the summer walking a thousand miles, starting at Land's End and heading wherever she heads. It's a very good idea; all students should do it. It should be part of their curriculum.

We discussed subjects of mutual interest, mostly around the tribulations of walking. I gave her two pieces of advice that will stand her in good stead on her walk through the path of life.

1. Philosophy is crap.
2. Always burst the blisters.

For good measure, I added a defensive weapon against our critics. (For some reason all walkers have critics.) Always remember that we are the normal ones. She seemed content with this advice and we carried on in opposite directions.

Ollie, of course, had no trouble finding the way anywhere. I eventually found the way out of Taunton with the kind advice of a runner, through various parks and wildlife trusts to the west of town, up the river and into the heartlands. The West Deane Way is clearly marked on the map but not in reality. Instead the A38 brought speedier travel and a footpath beside it to augment the chances of survival. Before Wellington, the Travelodge is very inviting.

Wellington itself seems a pleasant country town, full of some of the fattest people in England. I had a veggie breakfast there. Rolling countryside led up through hills and desirable villages. Garden centres appear to have replaced pubs as the destination for a British day out: get the motor out of the garage, drive into the country, stop at a garden centre, have a cup of tea and a cake and drive home again. What could be better?

Very clearly on the map, Tiverton Parkway lay just beyond the motorway, maybe a couple of hundred yards. Tired, I dawdled over tea and scones, allowing twenty minutes to walk there to catch the train. I crossed the motorway and reached the sign for the station - which said it was a mile away! Suddenly I was tired no longer. The station was two hundred yards away as the crow flies, but unless you could find a way down it was indeed a mile. I arrived streaming with sweat and generally a person you did not want to sit next to on the train.

Day 52: Tiverton Parkway to Tiverton to Withleigh
(10 July)

Can there really be a place called Noble Hindrance?

At last a canal!

I had thought it was too convoluted and had decided against it, but when it presented itself at Sampford Peverel it was just too hard to resist. It's the Grand Western Canal, originally planned to link the Bristol and English Channels but finally going from nowhere to nowhere. The first part was secluded. The sun shone, the ducks quacked, the moorhens squeaked, the sun still shone, it was idyllic. I came off at Halberton for a punnet of strawberries and intended to follow the road, but a friendly cyclist advised against it. In a word, she said: 'DON'T!!' So I went back to the canal.

Across it, a collection of tractors was warming up for an agricultural show next week. On the canal, a horse drawn barge disgorged a couple of dozen trippers. Almost everyone said hello. The exception was a strapping young woman in singlet and shorts, zoned in to the music in her ears and zooming past at three times my speed. Later she stood at a bus stop in Tiverton for the return journey. By that time she had probably been in the gym for a couple of hours.

A clutch of Tiverton's old buildings leads down to the River Eye. A plug must at this stage be put forward for the Angel Guesthouse. By the time I had dumped my bag and washed my face, they had printed out a map, a timetable and full walking instructions for Tiverton to Withleigh. They had also warned of the gradient on Baker's Hill.

It is steep. Then it leads to Long Drag Hill, which speaks for itself. Up there live the rich, in beautiful houses with massive views over brilliant Devon.

The strange thing about walking here is that the footpath went on as far as the last mansion; then it stopped. Who is it for? The rich people don't walk on it. It must be for the servants.

From there I stumbled through a couple of rough fields, scrambled down a ditch, scrambled up again and decided to take my chances on the road. From Withleigh I caught the bus back to Tiverton for the night.

As I set out this morning my Companion, who will spend the night photographing the installation of a gantry on the M25 - each to their own - said she hoped I enjoyed it.

'I'll enjoy having done it,' I said misanthropically.

She accused me of being perverse.

Well, who would enjoy walking along tarmac, avoiding the traffic, getting hot, bothered and knackered for far too long? The enjoyment lies in having done it, not in doing it.

Then I thought: actually, really, truly, today was great. Mostly. I've been to a part of the country I didn't know (and will never go to again). It's been beautiful. There has been pleasant interaction with various people. I speak the language. I drink the tea.

What more to ask?

Well, to reach a letter Q. But that's tomorrow.

Day 53: Withleigh to QUEEN DART to Witheridge
(11 July)

A man was standing in front of the sixty semi-derelict acres that he and his wife had just bought. He asked if I was lost. Very unusually, I wasn't.

Over the next hour we discussed, among other things:
Slurry
Sugar beet harvesting
Charles Dickens
Sustainable energy
Nuclear waste
PFIs
Loss of school playing fields
Rainforests
How many square yards in an acre (4,840)
How much is two-thirds of a pound (13 shillings and
    fourpence)
Rods, poles and perches
Timber framed houses
The Iraq War

I don't know his name but his son is Robert. They are working to transform this rundown small farm into a going concern. At the moment they're living in caravans.

A couple of miles earlier I had passed a farm claiming to be 'The Home of the Templeton Dexters'. I didn't know whether these were cattle or humans. ('Oh, are you one of the Kensington Dexters?' 'No, I'm one of the Templeton Dexters.') My new friend was able to give the disappointing news that they were cattle. He added: 'And they're not sinister either' - a joke so erudite that only the Latin educated could get it. It took me a while.

The road climbed steadily from Withleigh, then fell steeply down again to Templeton Bridge, a beauty spot indeed. The climb up again was nearly as bad as the descent. My knee went phut. I kept going and it improved. More hills, more valleys followed endlessly; undulating is always harder than one big climb and descent again. Views led from hills, streams ran through valleys. High above, a buzzard floated. Walking across deserts I have found this unfriendly but I don't think they'll be picking my bones in Devon. Across Witheridge Moor, the road burrowed into the woods like a tunnel.

My friend Phil had warned that Queen Dart was nothing at all, only a couple of houses, and he turned out to be absolutely right. There was Queen Dart House. There was Higher Queen Dart (or lower, I have already forgotten which). There was a tennis court. That was it. I think I have been swizzled several times over by the *A-Z Great Britain Road Atlas*. Like a number of its predecessor letter Qs, Queen Dart doesn't really exist at all.

I just caught the 2.13 bus from Witheridge to Exeter to see Phil. We had a coffee, then a pint, we reminisced and he went off to the cinema while I went home.

Phil told a story about a group of Probation clients he once took camping (in the days when there was a real Probation Service). They slept three to a tent and ate in these units. Unfortunately two of them didn't get a hot breakfast one morning in their tent. The third group member had sniffed all the gas in the night.

I don't know when I can come again. It could be weeks. Months.

Day 54: Witheridge to Copplestone
(25 September)

'Witheridge is closed,' said the bus driver. 'Did you know?'

Is it the plague? Have they been isolated?

They're working on the bridge. A shuttle bus dropped off passengers at Witheridge Square, from which they had to strike out alone.

Holidays are over. It has been months. Real life has to begin again. I girded up my loins and put my nose to the grindstone.

Rather than wait for a blue moon and a bus, I began the day with a cab from Tiverton Parkway station into Tiverton. The cabbie was Romanian, so we discussed my trip with Howard to Eforie Nord, near his home town, forty-five years ago. Then we got on to grammar. Why, he wanted to know, was English people's grammar so bad? Back home in Romania they teach grammar first. Here in England they only seem to teach it as an afterthought, as a specialisation. Why?

A man after my own heart.

From Witheridge I took back roads. Ahead and to the left was a line of hills. Is that Dartmoor? I have never been there, even to the prison. Morchard Bishop brought a decent footpath, the Two Moors Way, presumably Exmoor and Dartmoor. It rolled through Devon countryside until I lost it and found myself on the main road, the A377. At the junction there was a building to the right that I took little notice of. To the left were two unpleasant miles of main road, in the gathering twilight, hopping in and out of fields and hedges, leading to my planned destination of Copplestone.

I made it. Now where was The Devonshire Dumpling?

Not in Copplestone where it was supposed to be.

The first person said it was seven or eight miles to the north. But he was a Londoner. The next person said it was twenty minutes' walk away - back the way I had come.

It was thirty-five brisk minutes; two miles back along the road, making an extra four miles I had walked. It was totally dark and I arrived after eight o'clock. The Devonshire Dumpling was the building to the right of the junction of track and main road. I had walked right past it.

Isn't it reasonable, when they say it's in Copplestone, to deduce that it will indeed be in Copplestone?

Tomorrow I am staying in Okehampton at 65 Station Road. There isn't much doubt about that.

In the bar was a literary agent. How do I know he was a literary agent? Because he said so. His line of conversation followed that staple diet of agents: the ingratitude of their clients - going off to other agents after their career had been built, early books sold, foreign rights etc., etc.

Place name of the day: Morchard Bishop. Apparently Ernie Bevin went to school there.

A field of llamas gazed blankly at me.

Day 55: Copplestone to Okehampton
(26 September)

All of a sudden I turned a corner and there it was: a house called Westacre!

Now there is only one place in the country called Westacre and I live there. This house, then, was named after it, presumably by people who had lived there too. Who can it have been?

I rang the doorbell, provoking a cacophony of dog barking. An elderly (i.e. older than me) lady came to the door. I had probably interrupted her afternoon nap. I explained the situation. Could she tell me who had named the house Westacre?

She and her husband had lived there for sixteen years. Before them, a couple had lived there for nine years. She thought it was the people before that who had named the house.

This Sunday in our village hall in Westacre, Belinda Bush is organising a Macmillan fund raiser. A lot of old timers will be there so I will ask around. Who can it have been?

I thanked the lady and left. I think we had both enjoyed the chat.

At one time it seemed that I would reach Okehampton at about 2.30 and I began planning to go further in the day. In the event it was close to 6.30.

A morning of little lanes led to a spell on a dangerous A-road and then more little lanes, so little that they seemed likely to disappear altogether. Then the Tarka Trail led along the pretty River Taw; no otters though. I got lost once or twice, climbed gates, disturbed sheep and nearly got eaten by a mastiff on a chain. Bow was picturesque but rundown; half the houses were for sale or rent, the post office had closed and there wasn't a shop. In North Tawton I had beans on toast at Kirsty's Kitchen and discussed cakes. Taw Green was a hamlet of exclusivity. Okehampton is a very, very old fashioned sort of town - and probably proud of it.

Nearly fifty years ago I knew Liz from Okehampton. I don't remember her address and presume she doesn't still live here. I once visited her in Nairobi while passing through and staying in the youth hostel. Where is she now?

The blackberries are bountiful this year and further delayed my progress. Within a week or two they will be finished; the witch spits on them at Michaelmas and you must not eat them thereafter. Incidentally, farms used to change hands and the rents were paid at Michaelmas. Does this still apply?

My room last night had an interesting shower; right in the middle of the bedroom, all its sides were glass so that you were completely visible. I said nothing last night but discussed it with my landlady tonight. We speculated: it must be odd enough if you are sharing with a partner, but what if you are sharing the room with a friend?

Day 56: Okehampton to Castle Cross
(27 September)

If you want to know the way, ask a postman. They always know. In this case there was no bus stop marked on the map or in real life. He advised exactly where to stand but said it would stop anywhere if I flagged it down. I didn't share his confidence and stood instead at his invisible bus stop to find my way out.

I need to get home for tomorrow's Macmillan event, where I have a marrow in the guess-the-weight competition. Actually Colin grew it for me so I wouldn't claim the credit, but it's a monster.

After an hour and a half's walking a road sign stated, dispiritingly, that I had done only a mile from Okehampton. They must have the longest miles in the world round here. It continued like this, on the main road and the old railway line, for the rest of the morning. I wanted to get beyond Castle Cross but failed. Furthermore, it is difficult to know how far it is to the next place because for some reason the OS maps don't join up. Anyway, lying round the corner is another Q, Quoditch, so I shall look forward to that.

How can anywhere be called Bogtown? Or, for that matter, Germansweek?

Day 57: Castle Cross to QUODITCH
to Chapman's Well
(14 November)

Can there be any substance on earth stickier than Benylin? Spill some in your rucksack and see.

Torrential rain was forecast for two o'clock. I got off the bus at twelve and pushed on. It was a lot further than expected, not helped by missing a few turnings. There were hills; on the downhills my knee complained. And what was it all for? Well, Quoditch was there.

Then, in the blink of an eye, it was gone. Quoditch was a few big houses and a couple of barn conversions.

So what do they do, Quoditch residents? They farm or they commute. Or they convert barns. Or, of course, they run internet businesses from home. No-one was on the street anyway. The rain held off.

The theory was that it would grow dark later down here in the West. So much for theory. By the time I arrived at Ashwater, darkness was already falling. A diversion was welcome, in the shape of the village shop, post office and parish hall - all the same place, four years old, just what we want in Westacre. But it was growing ever darker. By the time I spent a hairy half hour on the main road there was no daylight left.

Chapman's Well provided sanctuary. Is the pub called the Arscott Arms? It didn't open till six but a tap on the window brought a sympathetic landlady who let me sit quietly for an hour, just before the heavens opened outside. The only way out of here was a taxi, so I ate mushrooms and garlic bread and read my book while waiting the two hours until one was free. Meanwhile a twenty-four-hour pool competition started in aid of prostate cancer treatment; most of the village had someone who had suffered from it and most of the village was there.

My taxi driver has a two-week-old baby. He was very foul mouthed (the driver not the baby) and a very good driver.

I looked at hotels in Launceston on the internet. There appeared to be thirty-five hotels in Launceston, many of them great concrete monstrosities. What? In Launceston? Ah yes. There's also Launceston, Tasmania. Apparently it is not unusual for punters to turn up here with a hotel booking for Tasmania.

Good to see the Conservative Club is boarded up.

Day 58: Chapman's Well to Pensilva
(15 November)

Two hundred and thirty seven marathons...

A marathon is taking place here tomorrow and one of the participants is in the bar. In fact two are in the bar; but the younger brother is a wimp who has done only a hundred or so. They are both busy taking on liquid; cider is apparently the most useful.

I started the day back at Chapman's Well, where the twenty-four-hour pool game would still be going on. I didn't look in to see if I had won the raffle. There was a long way to go.

Further than I thought.

The bridge over the Tamar led to Cornwall, where surely, as the westernmost county, it would stay light later in the day... That one still didn't work unfortunately.

Yesterday they forecast rain and it stayed fine. Today they forecast fine and...

It is extraordinarily difficult to put on waterproof trousers over walking boots. It probably isn't if you're young but I don't remember that far back. In a bus shelter I contorted myself for twenty frustrating minutes.

It took two or three hours to reach Launceston, a town on a hill with a little round castle on top. In the town information centre Alison and I discussed the world - the Caribbean, walking, Istanbul and the Cornish coastal path. Then she booked me accommodation for the night, just the way they used to.

I thought it was eleven miles away and I would do it in three hours. In fact it was fourteen miles away and it took five hours, the last hour and a half of them in pitch dark. Then the place was full of crazy marathoners.

We are right under Bodmin Moor. Behind us is Mount Caradon, with a big radio mast on it. The landlady keeps pigs, chickens and quails. Apparently you kill a quail by snipping its head off. Yes, thank you very much.

I never knew Cornwall had so many rivers. They are all over the place and, as Alison said in the tourist office, 'none of it is downhill'. Strictly this cannot be true, of course, but the downhills are as steep and as painful as the uphills and all the rivers run north/south while I was walking east/west. Altogether today was a knackering twenty miles.

Place name of the day: Broadwoodwidger. Runner up: Bathpool.

Day 59: Pensilva to QUETHIOCK to Liskeard
(16th November)

The question was whether I could walk from the guesthouse through Quethiock to Liskeard in time for my train. The landlord said no. I made it with five minutes to spare after a dash through town.

The stragglers were just starting out on the marathon. Without being unkind, some of them looked as if they might struggle with twenty-six yards, never mind twenty-six miles. It was definitely the taking part that counted.

Through Pensilva the road led to St Ive (not St Ives) and then, yes, Quethiock (pronounced Quithick). That's two letter Qs in three days, yippee, life is for living!

So what's it like in Quethiock (pronounced Quithick)? I had been told that there was nothing in Quethiock, but this is unfair. I saw two people moving. Very, very slowly. That was it, it seemed, until a woman shot past with a dog. What sort of people live here? From the quirky pronunciation of their village I assumed that they were elusive, cautious folk, trying to fool the invading enemy into thinking they were in a place called Quethiock when in fact they were in Quithick. Or perhaps they just can't spell. I never found out.

Liskeard seemed ok. On my trip home I sat next to Gavin, who was off to work in the film industry in Vancouver for two years. He's a computer animator so I didn't understand a word. His father is a farmer so that was better.

Day 60: Liskeard to Lostwithiel
(6 December)

The 7.22 from Paddington was eager to start. We on board were all eager to start. But until they sorted out the points failure at Langley no-one was going anywhere.

Then, when they sorted out that one, there was another one at Reading.

They got that sorted out but then there was a bus replacement between Plymouth and Liskeard. A passenger strongly resembling Sonny Bono on a bad day made a beeline and sat next to me.

It was one o'clock before I set off. Within two minutes I took my first wrong turning.

Then it was up and down all their bloody valleys in bloody Cornwall. Down up, down up. After a few miles my map expired and the only thing to do was take the main road, the A390. It was tedious having to jump into the bank all the time but not as tedious as getting lost.

At last, however, the benefit of western-ness has kicked in. On a clear night it wasn't pitch dark until after five o'clock, an hour later than in Norfolk, and I was in the pub by half past. Later, a woman in the bar apologised for smelling of goat; she had been working with them all day and at one stage had to wrestle one. And, she said, they do smell of goat.

Sitting on a delayed train inevitably brings thoughts of wasted life. Then come thoughts of age. A couple of days ago I went to watch Norfolk's leading tennis players, Richard and Olivia, in a tournament in Nottingham. Tournament director was Richard Joyner, once a Norfolk boy, now a much respected official. I first played with the second Richard when he was thirteen and I was thirty. Now he is fifty... We had a good chat. Tempus fugit. Carpe Diem. All those old Latin things. Soon

I shall be looking back and thinking: 'Oh, I wish I was sixty-seven again and could walk down a dangerous main road in Cornwall hoping to get indoors somewhere before it gets dark or snows or I get hit by a bus or collapse with a bad knee or curse yet another bloody Cornish valley.'

Place name of the day: Catchfrench.

Day 61: Lostwithiel to St Austell
(7 December)

'The people of Lostwithiel think they're special!'

The woman leaned out of her window and confided again: 'People in Lostwithiel think they're special!'

In case there should still be any doubt, bold writing on a number of sheets of paper was taped to her windows: 'The people of Lostwithiel think they're special!'

Lostwithiel is quaint and slightly decaying and has hotels, pubs and novelty shops. It is down in another bloody valley. The Eden Project keeps it busy and passing trade keeps it ticking over, but neither of these is the main attraction. This is the Park Sunday Market that could be seen from the moon. They said in Lostwithiel that it is market day today. And every other day, I bet. The car park is bigger than a farm and the market itself could house a fleet of airliners. I didn't go in.

On the edge of St Austell a popular bakery was besieged by customers wanting scones, pasties and lunch. One of the staff wrote out directions for the station without which I would be walking still. I had a cheese and onion pasty, holding it by the crust on top, the traditional grip of the tin miners to avoid their dirty hands getting on the bit they were eating.

In the distance are conical hills, like miniature Alps. Presumably they are slag heaps from the old tin mines. Every now and again someone tries to revive the old mines but it doesn't last long. Their only lasting purpose is as a tourist attraction.

Over a hill, there lies the sea for the first time on the trip. (The Thames Estuary and the horrible bit on the Isle of Sheppey don't count.) I know people in Cornwall but won't inflict myself on them on this journey.

Day 62: St Austell to QUINTRELL DOWNS
(31 December)

For a couple of weeks I have had an infected toe. I took it to the doctor. This means that I am now taking:

Heart pills
Parkinson's pills
Vitamin pills
Glucosamine
Antibiotics

Oh, and a cream for a fungal condition but we won't go into that. (It's not what you think.)

Today I met a man from the South Tyrol. He had been walking the accursed Cornish Coastal Path, which he agreed was a spectacular nightmare. It had done for his knee and he was hobbling along the road for a rest. He was surprised that I knew where the South Tyrol was and even more surprised that I had walked through his home town forty-three years ago when he was one year old.

All this delayed me and I tore into Quintrell Downs, latest of the Qs, to catch the 5.28 to Roche. At St Austell tourist information the nice old boy (younger than me) advised me sagaciously that Newquay, just beyond Quintrell Downs, was for young people on New Year's Eve; and I had already discovered that on this date the Travelodge Newquay cost literally five times as much as the Travelodge Roche. So I aimed for the train to Roche, to return in the morning.

I missed it by ten seconds. The barrier came down and I couldn't get across the road.

Oh well. The next train was due in two hours. I would have a pint and some grub in the pub.

Two problems arose. First, the pub was shut, preparing for New Year's Eve. Second, the train in two hours didn't stop at Roche. And the one in four hours' time wasn't running at all. And there were lots of buses but none of them went to Roche. (Sardonically pronounced with an acute accent on the 'e', by the way.) So finally I did a deal with a taxi driver who was heading that way.

On Christmas Day I still needed to read four books by 31 December to reach my annual target of fifty. I found three very short books but today, because of all the delays, I have failed to finish the very good book by Malcolm Mackay given to me for Christmas by my friend Judy.

So Quintrell Downs is the furthest letter Q of all. It was dark when I got there. What was the walk like from St Austell? Tedious.

Day 63: QUINTRELL DOWNS to Roche
(1 January)

It seemed scarcely believable that I should miss another train. I never miss trains. The station was, I was reliably informed, two minutes from the Travelodge. So it was. Unfortunately I didn't set out on the right two minutes. By the time I had done a complete circuit of a trading estate I knew the train had gone.

So I stooped again to the last refuge of the scoundrel. Instead of taking the train back to Quintrell Downs and walking to Roche, I walked it in reverse: Roche to Quintrell Downs. It's a disgrace.

As punishment, I spent the day walking into a strong wind instead of walking with it. As another punishment, I set off in totally the wrong direction (again) and walked an extra couple of miles. I deserved it.

The old A30 is now a footpath over Goss Moor, known locally as The Goss. Before it was the A30 it was Roman. Before that, it was prehistoric. It has been around.

In an excellent pub, The Blue Anchor, an ebullient young man brought my cup of tea. I said he was very perky for New Year's Day. I'm always perky, he said, whatever the date.

The back roads led to Mountjoy and a big green road. (Green on the map, that is.) Then here was Quintrell Downs again. What does it look like in daylight? Better in the dark, I'm afraid.

Place name of the day: Trebilcock. Runner up: Goonbarrow Junction.

I know people in Penzance, Falmouth, Redruth and Port Isaac and would happily spend an evening with any of them. (Whether they would feel the same is another matter, of course.) Foolishly, I haven't seen any of them but am now turning round from my furthest point in Cornwall.

Day 64: Roche to Bodmin Parkway
(2 January)

I made the mistake tonight of looking up where all those Qs are. Maybe I hadn't rigorously researched it before setting off. Shropshire, for example, is festooned with them (well, at least four). I knew that. What I hadn't realised is that one of them is about a million miles from the other three. One in Lancashire has to be in bloody Blackpool; since they took away Furness from Lancs and gave it to Cumbria, this is as far as you can go. Then there seems to be one in Northants that I simply hadn't spotted before.

In March this venture will have been going on for two years. Can I live long enough to complete it?

More immediately, it's hard to work out the best route to wherever-it-is between Bristol and Bath that's the next Q. I don't want to retrace my steps but nor do I want to go on a massive detour. A bit of planning is called for.

Today was straightforward. Minor roads led towards Bodmin then veered off into the woods. The last part lay through a large holiday area that I can't remember the name of and can't read on the map. Ah, Lanhydrock, can that be right? A massive forested estate led down a very steep hill to Bodmin Parkway station where - even better - a superb little buffet served me with a two-egg bap.

I don't want to climb up that hill again next time.

Day 65: Bodmin Parkway to Liskeard
(31 January)

It was the Day of Generosity. It will be followed tomorrow by the Day of Atonement.

All day people kept offering me lifts. Obviously I declined them all. Well, I would do normally. This time, as an absolute total exception, I accepted help very briefly, on the understanding that I would more than make up for it tomorrow.

There is no obvious way for the walker to exit Bodmin Parkway towards Liskeard. Nobody had any idea. Three elderly people (i.e. as old as me) insisted on giving me a lift for about a hundred yards to the junction, but that doesn't really count, does it? Which way could I avoid the A38 and reach Liskeard before dark?

I had started the day in Todmorden, Yorkshire. Even leaving very early, a glance at the map will reveal a problem: it's a very long way and the chances of finishing in daylight are remote.

On a short path by the river I met a man exercising his dogs and we had a long and fruitful chat about the situation. He decided there was only one solution, via Mount and St Neot on the back roads. First he would give me a lift up the hill to show me the junction.

Obviously I declined as usual. No I didn't, and there were three reasons:

(i) If I didn't accept I would get lost
(ii) He wouldn't take no for an answer
(iii) I was a worthless human being

It was probably about a mile and I would atone. I set out for Mount and St Neot.

Around this time I was supposed to meet my friend Deborah from Falmouth. It turns out that most of her ancestors were buried in St Neot. Due to my incompetence we didn't manage to meet but I had a cup of tea in a very nice pub in St Neot and by the time I left there it was 6.30 and dark.

This darkness thing is becoming a part of the picture. On back roads with no traffic it isn't a problem. A long and lovely valley led up from St Neot. At least, in daylight it is probably long and lovely. It was followed by a spell on the A38 because I took a wrong turning but then, Bob's your uncle, I was in Doublebois. A short cut led to a dead end in an industrial estate but then it was on to Dobwalls. Finally, just out of town, I asked the way.

At 8.30 on Saturday night there weren't any post people so I asked a deliverer of Chinese takeaways. He turned out to be a calibration engineer, just finishing his apprenticeship and supplementing his income with a night per week on deliveries. He said he had seen me earlier in the evening, probably several times. He not only showed me the way but took me there.

Everyone I met today was friendly, helpful and generous. The problem with Cornwall is not the people but the bloody valleys. Down and up, down and up, they never stop. The man who gave me the earlier lift said that people from Norfolk came in their new Skodas which immediately indicated malfunctions on the dashboard. First thing in the morning, for example, it can't believe it has to wake up and climb a hill so it thinks something is wrong and a flashing light comes on. Of course, the story may be apocryphal. Furthermore, it is a myth that Norfolk is flat. You should see Tumbley Hill.

Yorkshire was covered in snow this morning. Cornwall was covered in hailstones tonight.

I shall atone for the lift by walking round Liskeard to get a coffee tomorrow.

Day 66: Liskeard to St Ann's Chapel
(1 February)

Steep hills and back roads took up most of the day. One spot suddenly seemed familiar; it was only a mile from Quethiock and I had been there before. I sped off in the opposite direction. It would really have pissed me off if I had hit a Q for the second time when it takes me all my time trying to reach them the first time.

A steep, steep footpath led to Callington, then another long climb led to, well, the top. Behind lay Bodmin Moor, not far from the venue of the 237 marathon man a few weeks ago. Ahead lay Dartmoor. Overnight the whole of Cornwall was bathed in snow. It melted quickly in the morning except on Dartmoor, where it stayed all day.

On the road from Callington two fat ladies walked towards me. That is a discriminatory statement in multiple ways. Be that as it may, they did. As they drew level, it was almost impossible to resist crying out: 'EIGHTY EIGHT! BINGO!' But I did. Resist it, that is.

Another long climb led to St Ann's Chapel, a grim little place with fine views. I had a very bad meal there. My experience of vegetable lasagne is a wide one, since every establishment in the country offers it as their vegetarian option. Surprisingly often, it is very good. Surprisingly often, it is very bad. This one was the latter surprise. Vegetable lasagne surprise.

I contacted my friend Phil to see if he could meet me tomorrow, which he couldn't. I'm not doing very well with my last minute efforts to see old friends. Perhaps I should give them more than a day's notice.

Day 67: St Ann's Chapel to Tavistock
(2 February)

It was a short day but not short enough.

Exactly what sort of a place is this Tavistock then? For some reason it is a World Heritage Site. Sir Francis Drake came from here. Nineteenth-century mining brought affluence, squalor and building. But can they provide a tourist office?

Oh yes, everyone including town hall staff knew where the tourist office was: it's in the archway. The trouble is: it's not. It is now in an alcove in the Spar shop. The Spar shop has also taken over the post office. Anything else it could franchise? The police? The hospital? The Queen?

If it did, let's hope it employs living people. The tourist office employs only leaflets. One of these, the guide to the town, is perhaps the most useless tourist map ever devised. It has lots of numbers indicating various establishments but it omits to say what they are. Perhaps it's an economy measure.

Gunnislake and the Tamar river were (probably still are) at the bottom of a big hill, almost a gorge. This is the border between Cornwall and Devon. I got vertigo on the bridge, then it was up and down then like the proverbial yoyo (or honeymoon couple).

The museum employs a Paranormal Analysis Team.

Day 68: Tavistock to Princetown
(15 February)

'Aim for the mast,' said my landlady on the phone, 'if it's clear. From there you can come straight down to the town.'

Ah yes. If it's clear while wandering around Dartmoor in the growing dark you can walk straight down. I can get lost on a postage stamp, I don't need the wilds of Dartmoor. I stuck to the road. As it happened she drove past and stopped and we identified ourselves. She runs the B&B and has two thousand hectares of sheep and cattle moorland. That's one hell of a lot of hectares.

A long climb, a swoop down and a much longer climb led to the top. Dartmoor was vast, bleak and beautiful. Ancient rock formations fell around. Ponies run wild, taking little notice of car loads of Sunday trippers wanting to befriend them. A snipe flew past. At least, I think it was a snipe. Along with peewits, thrushes and bullfinches they no longer appear in Norfolk, victims of the modern world.

Princetown is a small, remarkable town, dominated entirely by the massive HM Prison Dartmoor. Apparently the prison is due to close, in which case Princetown will become a ghost town. It is plain, austere, immaculate and soulless, like a military garrison town. A visitors' centre, a prison museum, a couple of pubs and some cafés have been dotted around but make little impact. I bet the environmental allowance is astronomical to induce prison officers to work here.

In the pub I took exception to the boss man (he certainly thought he was the boss man). The reason is too trivial to repeat but I certainly won't be going back. He nearly spoiled an amazing day.

Day 69: Princetown to Moretonhampstead
(16 February)

I woke up, looked at the clock and leaped out of bed. It was 8.15! I looked again. Oh no, it wasn't 8.15 it was 2.40. Easy to get them confused. I slunk back into bed again.

On the road back into Princetown a very determined man was climbing slowly up the hill with walking poles. We talked. Just before he left the army he was struck down with rheumatoid arthritis. From nowhere, he became totally incapacitated. At one moment he was exercising with his Marines, the next moment he was looking at wheelchair sports. Behind a brave exterior he was devastated.

Archery he had found to be calming and therapeutic. Wheelchair tennis he had done a bit of. I suggested he tried coaching others with disabilities: not just physical disabilities but also learning disabilities, which is crying out for coaches with commitment. He said this was really something to think about. I hope he follows this up.

There was more, much more, of Dartmoor. What a vast, inscrutable area, bleak beyond bleak. Up went the road on a climb, then a downward swoop, then a longer climb again. Sheep, sheep and more sheep. Swathes of moorland. At the top a north wind blew up a sudden hailstorm. It was short, painful and gone again. A sixteen per cent descent brought a gentler world with a more benevolent climate.

Dartmoor is littered with paths but, like the valleys, they all seem to run north to south. I am going west to east; am I the only one? I stuck to the road through Two Bridges and Postbridge (now why were they called...?) where a cup of tea saved the day. It was a hard session which eventually brought Moretonhampstead, a sort of Hampstead without the heath, where an excellent scone next door to the information tourist office pursued the cup down my eager gob.

Day 70: Moretonhampstead to Exeter
(5 April)

I had a big toenail removed. That's my excuse for an absence of nearly two months. It is now over two years since I started this venture. I am not even halfway. I never imagined it would take two years, let alone the rest of my life.

There's a GP at my surgery, a very nice man, who specialises in toenail removal. They're all very keen on it. You have to make absolutely clear at your appointment that your earache, tonsillitis or heart failure are totally unconnected to your big toe and you really, really do not want your nail removed. Is it my imagination or are there a lot of people in Swaffham limping?

But my surgery is excellent and the service I have had from them is unsurpassed.

Anyway, the details of my toenail removal are unpleasant so I will just say that there was no question of my going anywhere for a few weeks.

I have been reading a book about Parkinson's. Apparently dragging one foot is caused by weakness in the other and a failure to bounce the ball of the foot. I tried it today and it's true.

The day was spellbinding: England at its best. A perfect, cloudless April sky shone on a world of daffodils and primroses, the most I have ever seen. The scenery was spectacular, the first half still in the Dartmoor National Park, steep and bare, the second half still hilly and verdant. In fact it was a bit too spectacular for my liking. For a reborn ingrowing toenail the long hills were a nasty baptism of fire.

Allegedly it was twelve miles but actually it was a couple more. Phil was waiting in Exeter and was on his second pint by the time I got there. He has a policy, if he doesn't know a place, of trying it out with fish and chips. If I ate fish I might have done the same because the Vegetable Wellington was disgusting. However, we caught up with the world. Phil is deaf and I have voice problems and a man in the bar brayed throughout the evening, but we did our best to communicate.

Day 71: Exeter to Whimple
(6 April)

Exeter is a fine city. Unfortunately I didn't see much of it as I took a foolish short cut out of the city, walked several extra miles and got in a bad mood. In addition I failed to reach my target for the day, Honiton, from which I had a train booked at 2.55. Finally I had to catch a bus from Whimple to make it.

But the bus passed a second hand bookshop in Honiton and in consolation I bought a very obscure cricket book. The day was not absolutely wasted.

Not much else to say. Must do better.

Day 72: Whimple to Honiton
(6 May)

What kind of a name is Whimple anyway? It's neither a wimp nor a winkle. I looked it up in the dictionary. Oh, it's an alternative spelling of wimple. It can also mean 'a crafty twist'. Does this sum up the nuns who wore it?

Whimple itself doesn't have anything to say for itself. I got off the bus and carried on.

By chance I had some work in Exeter today so I took the opportunity to double up and save myself a train fare. That worked out as well as most of my plans. Honiton took ages to get to - three hours against the two planned - and I missed the train and had to buy a ticket for myself after all. Then I thought I was buying a period return when in fact it was a day return, so I can't even use it to come back again. Apart from the next walk, I am never coming back to Honiton.

It's a picturesque little town too.

I didn't get there in time to buy another obscure cricket book from Honiton Books or even some food from one of the many takeaways. I was hungry, I was thirsty and I was not in a sweet mind. Would there be hot food on the evening train?

I scanned the menu on the food trolley. Hot food? Yes, they had hot food: they had porridge.

Porridge?

Well, I'd better have some then. The attendant, who was not British by birth, held up a carton and read the details in consternation. Did I really want this? He clearly thought I was a lunatic. Hmmm. Luke warm water on some oat flakes. Not quite as tickety-boo as I had hoped but it staved off starvation on the slow train from Honiton to Waterloo. Just. I read Henry Marsh's book about brain surgery and felt happy that I had never had to slice open anyone's skull to remove a tumour, or indeed for any other reason.

Day 73: Honiton to Churchinford
(12 May)

I failed to bring: sun glasses; hat; waterproof trousers. So, whatever the weather, I was screwed.

The tourist office in Honiton gave brusque directions. Apparently tourist offices nowadays charge a fiver to find accommodation. They don't do it across county borders either. So I went off bedless for Churchinford. They did look it up on the internet, though, and said the pub there had lots of accommodation.

Really there is nowhere in the world as beautiful as England in May. I said that last year. Within England, Norfolk is of course the loveliest part of the kingdom but Devon and Somerset make a valiant effort. Bluebells, daisies, buttercups and dandelions festoon the banks of the roads. Everywhere is deep green.

Up through a stunning valley, Luppitt arrived uneventfully: a series of grass fields waiting to be cut for hay. The pub was central. Would it like to give me a bed for the night?

No.

But it says...

The information on the internet is apparently 'historic'. Does that mean that, like an old castle or palace, no-one is going to change it?

They gave me some numbers and I finished in a very, very comfortable establishment on the road to Taunton. They keep alpacas. The proprietor picked me up and will take me back again tomorrow morning. I may even have a couple of hours' work tomorrow which will help to pay for the exorbitant accommodation.

Day 74: Churchinford to Taunton
(13 May)

All roads lead to Taunton. So do all trains, buses and even the canal. Taunton rests in a bowl surrounded by hills, a little bit like Innsbruck or Kathmandu. A very little bit.

The road descended from the Black Down Hills. On the other side of town are the Quantocks. I hope to miss them.

I did a couple of hours' work with my contact in Taunton in a very nice café then caught the train.

This Parkinson's business is a bit of a pain in the arse. (Actually that's about the only symptom it doesn't offer.) Various books offer alternatives to traditional medical treatment (pills). Most of the alternatives have something going for them; only a few verge on the crackpot. One particular remedy seems to fit the bill for everyone. What is it? Walking!

It's not quite as simple as that. It demands a certain style of walking and a certain speed which I definitely can't match at the moment. I am also supposed to do breathing exercises, rotational exercises, back muscle exercises and most other exercises you've never heard of. Some of them I do, some of them I'm too lazy for (idiot). One that I am prepared to do is walking.

But if walking is so good for Parkinson's, why have I got it? On the other hand, how bad would I have been if I hadn't been walking?

All these exercises only treat the symptoms, not the cause. If they make you better, though, who cares what they do?

Day 75: Taunton to Bridgwater
(10 June)

'DANGER. GIANT HOGWEED.'

Head for the hills!

Fortunately we were well defended by a line of Second World War pillboxes built regularly along the path.

The Taunton-Bridgwater canal lay, unsurprisingly, between Taunton and, yes, you guessed it.

On the towpath I met a seventy-six-year-old, out for his afternoon constitutional. We discussed canals, crops, cutbacks, computers, cyclists and canoeing. Somehow we didn't get on to cricket. Later, in a towpath café, two women of a certain age were making plans; whether it was for the future or for the day was unclear. Then one of them said loudly: 'WHAT YOU WANT IS A GIN PALACE!'

On a day like this, on a towpath, I acknowledge everyone coming the other way - walker, cyclist, child, dog, fishermen (those bastards). Fifty per cent give a cheery greeting in return. The other half think I'm mad.

The heart leaps on finding a canal, which will be flat, straight, easy and traffic free. The problem with canals is that they are also excruciatingly boring. They don't sound boring: water, trees, boats, locks. Then more water, trees, boats, locks... It's a bit like Finland, which has five thousand lakes. This is nice, you think: trees and water, trees and water. Then more trees and water, more...

A friendly woman, out for a walk while her daughter did Brownies, guided me into Bridgwater. We talked about dyslexia.

Later in the pub it was said that there are four times as many woodpeckers as usual this year. Fewer swallows and swifts, absolutely no cuckoos but four times as many woodpeckers.

Day 76: Bridgwater to Street
(11 June)

Cold pizza for breakfast. Yummy.

Bridgwater, says everyone, is a risky place. Don't go out after dark. If possible don't go out at all. It used to have docks. The canal was built to take coal one way, wool the other. What does it take now? Dunno.

It didn't go my way unfortunately. Last night everyone in the bar fell over themselves to give helpful instructions for today, some of which I followed. The route was obscure, circuitous and strange. This appears to be the Somerset Levels.

No-one outside Somerset had ever heard of the Somerset Levels until they were flooded. Most of the land looks below sea level. Enormous drains, like rivers, scythe across it in a network of dykes. Much of it is wetland; sheep or cattle graze some of it. The map shows a ridge of hills surrounding a plethora of blue lines. Wander in there and you might never wander out again.

By great good fortune I arrived in Street just in time for the bus to Castle Cary and the train out. By lesser good fortune the bus didn't come. Apparently this is a common occurrence and a collection of vultures, known as taxi drivers, waits across the road for the non-appearance. My vulture was the very agreeable Steve and we talked football. He also told me that his best ever day's business was four separate trips to Heathrow. He was collecting four members of the German royal family (ex) and they were obliged, or chose, to travel entirely separately. It would probably suit quite a lot of families.

Thirty-five or so years ago Norfolk men's tennis team used to come here to play Millfield School on the Saturday and then Somerset on the Sunday: we generally won the first match and lost the second. Millfield in those days produced most of the country's best young tennis players - and a fair number of cricketers, rugby players and anything else you care to mention. To go there if you didn't have one of those scholarships, you had to be rich.

Day 77: Street to Wookey Hole (!)
(but via Glastonbury and Wells...)
(16 June)

Place name of the day: no contest.

Castle Cary station, out in the wilds, was semi-deserted as usual. Next week 15,000 people will descend on it. The Glastonbury Festival is nigh.

Do local people go to the festival? The man in charge of the station: 'My Baden Powell days are over.' His mate stopping by: 'I don't know how you ever find your own tent.' So a straw poll suggests not.

The bus from Castle Cary to Street had one major advantage over the bus from Street to Castle Cary: it came. Street looked much as I had left it. A couple of miles over the drain lay Glastonbury.

On the right is Glastonbury Tor, a hill with a ruin on top. People come to worship there. The town itself is really ok, with an abbey, a market and a host of hostelries. Languidly the punters filled the cafés and nobody was in a hurry.

Over another drain, the cycle path followed the main road back into the Levels, then struck directly into the wetlands (drained). Much of the land is half wild; it must contain more insects than the rest of the south of England. Families of swans live privately. Hills all round create an enclave. Out of it stems Wells.

Huge cathedral. Massive grounds. A very pleasant tourist town. My friend Chris was waiting and we spent three hours catching up over numerous cups of tea. He has a book coming out about Zulus and is researching another about Comanches. And he has a new grandchild. There was much more from both of us. He gave me a bottle of homemade elderflower cordial and I went off looking for Wookey Hole.

The West Mendip Way led into beautiful countryside but unfortunately not to Wookey Hole. Luckily I bumped into a couple walking their dog who told me this, otherwise I might still be there.

Wookey Hole appears to be famous but I haven't discovered what for.

Day 78: Wookey Hole to Midsomer Norton
(17 June)

It is now many walking days and even more calendar days since I walked through a place beginning with Q. People say to me: 'But there's no letter Q round here' and they're right. When I can say, 'Oh, but there's a Q coming up tomorrow' I feel vindicated. When, however, I say, 'Oh, there's one in about a hundred miles' they look at me strangely. Still, that's their problem.

Now I am bearing down on Queen Charlton. I am reminded of that terrible acronym for measuring success: SMART. I can only remember one of the words, Measurable.

Stupid. Anal. Retentive. Terrifying.

The day started badly. A couple of seriously obese customers ate the largest breakfast I have ever seen. All day, fat people stuffed fat food into their fat mouths. It was reminiscent of North American holidaymakers breakfasting on a stack of pancakes plus eggs (sunny side up) plus sausage plus hash browns etc. before getting into their cars. But they were North Americans, you expect that kind of thing. These were British. British and obese.

Out of Wookey Hole, a stiff climb led into the Mendips. Behind lay the view to Glastonbury Tor and beyond. Ahead lay mist - the tops were covered in cloud. The Monarch's Way - haven't we seen that before? At the top, dogs were taking their people for a walk on the moorland. A series of minor roads led to Chewton Mendip.

Somehow I have reached an area not covered by any of my Ordnance Survey maps; it's just off the corner of all of them. However, the café in Chewton Mendip combined excellent directions with the finest tea cakes in the West Country and Midsomer Norton was reached in mid-afternoon. It looks like a poor town.

Day 79: Midsomer Norton to Stanton Wick
(13 July)

Actually Midsomer Norton isn't such a bad place. It was once a coalmining town and a slag heap remains as a reminder. The young snack bar entrepreneur in the town centre is a Bristol Rovers supporter; today they lost a legal battle with Sainsbury's about redevelopment. He reminded me that Norwich City once played the nearby Paulton Rovers in the cup. Paulton is no more than a village. Fortunately we did manage to sort them out. (Dublin, Huckerby.)

Heavy murk brought near dark by 3.30. Light drizzle fell; so did medium drizzle and heavy drizzle. A man with a pram put me right in Glatton and sent me past big houses, an old mill and various unspecified works. I took a Great British Footpath which, needless to say, soon became a Great British Disappearance. And it was wet.

Q

My only direct connection with the mining industry lay in a correspondence with Arthur Scargill. At that time Scargill was the devil incarnate to the politicians and their tame newspapers. My group in our trade union resolved to give him a bit of a morale boost so I wrote to him and asked if he would like to become president of the union. (The position was vacant. The furore would have been global. 'Probation officers appoint Satan!') No answer came so I rang him up. I got his secretary who explained that three-quarters of their mail was intercepted and never arrived. She invited me to write to Scargill at her home address instead.

Sadly, our venture went nowhere. I wrote. Scargill wrote back and thanked us for our good wishes but said that unfortunately he was not allowed to accept a post with any other union.

Day 80: Stanton Wick to QUEEN CHARLTON to Keynsham
(14 July)

'THAT'S KEYNSHAM – SPELLED K-E-Y-N-S-H-A-M.'

To everyone - but everyone - of a certain age, the word Keynsham means only one thing. Horace Batchelor, resident of Keynsham, had a system with which he could win the pools. So too could you if you sent him a postal order and he sent you his system. Day after day, week after week he advertised on Radio Luxembourg. There was only one flaw in the scenario as he presented it. If he had had the success that he claimed, he wouldn't be living in Keynsham.

Somehow, between last night and this morning, I have lost my map. I am left with the small scale road map book of the whole country which, even with my glasses, I can't read. Instead of a map I had to ask the way every few minutes. It was tricky too. First, everyone knew the way to the next village but no-one knew the way beyond. Second, a serious shortage of signposts made the area a bit like central Norfolk. If you don't know where you are, you've got no right to be there.

Villages came and went with no sign of Queen Charlton until a lady in a graveyard (a living lady) showed me the way. Queen Charlton appeared. Wow.

No-one went to Queen Charlton to do their Christmas shopping. Or to go on a bender (though there are plenty of bends). If you want to buy a very, very large stone-built house, though, and live in a hamlet with stone walls on all sides, this is the place for you. It is far and away the most impressive letter Q so far, all dozen or so houses of it. There are even a few houses for the poor, although it is doubtful whether the poor live there now.

It was hilly and it was hard. I wandered down into Keynsham (spelled K...), found the station and went to sleep. I intended to go much further today but just couldn't be bothered. No doubt this would put me behind schedule but fortunately there isn't a schedule.

I now have to return to Wiltshire. It was miles out of the way previously so I ignored it; it is still miles out of the way. For preference I would pop into Bristol and straight up the road to Gloucester. Instead I have to go to Bath, then miles back into Wiltshire and then back again to Gloucester. It will be character forming.

Day 81: Chippenham to Bath
(4 August)

Shouldn't that be Keynsham to Bath?

I was in the toilet when the bus rolled out of Chippenham station. That was my excuse for throwing principles out of the window.

The plan was to walk from Keynsham to Chippenham. In practice I had doubts as to whether I could do that but the spirit was willing. So I got a ticket for Bath, to get the connection to Keynsham.

But the trains weren't going to Bath. Well, some of them were, but they were going all the way to Bristol and then coming back again to Bath (passing through Keynsham but not stopping there). If you wanted Bath direct, you got the bus.

Unless you were in the toilet.

It was hours until the next one. Sod that. I had to resort again to the last refuge of the scoundrel. I would walk it in the opposite direction.

So I meandered along a series of zigzag roads and the occasional footpath, lengthy but undemanding, from Chippenham to Bath through a succession of stone villages (or stoned villages, they were so quiet): Easton, Neston, Kingsdown and Bath. Doing it in the wrong direction meant that it was downhill into Bath.

Here, the road passed endless beautiful West Country stone terraces. Most of them are now multiple occupancy but some have been refurbished into family homes again. I reached the station just in time to miss the train going in the wrong direction.

I haven't forgotten the bit from Keynsham to Bath. I will fill it in later.

Day 82: Chippenham to Calne
to QUEMERFORD to Calne
(17 August)

It started badly.

From my bedroom window at home came a thud. Too slowly, I realised that a bird had flown into it. It lay stunned in the road, a spotted woodpecker - and a cat sat watching it. I flew down in dressing gown and slippers, inevitably too late. The cat had got it. A sad cry came from the woodpecker. I chased the cat but it made off, bird in mouth.

I hate cats. On an individual basis I get on fine with them but people should stop keeping them. They kill more birds than pesticides and natural predators combined.

That was Norfolk. In London I was late for lunch with Michael, Morna, Jackie, Cyril and Layton due to circumstances beyond my control, but they were forgiving. Cyril bought my soup and dropped me at the tube station. He's a good lad.

Chippenham: have I been here before? Ah yes, two weeks ago. I couldn't remember a thing. It seems pleasant enough, with the traditional charity shops and bookies dominating the High Street. The way out of town was clear enough, eventually finding a cycle path on the route of an old railway line, a pleasant spot to spend a summer evening surrounded by walkers, runners, cyclists and dogs - but no cats. I hate cats.

On the edge of Calne stands Quemerford, so I wandered down until I reached - well, what did I reach? To the right was a small river with an old mill, ahead was a post office. Was that all? There was no indication that anyone had arrived in Quemerford. Or anywhere else. A street was called Quemerford. Oh, another of them. I hope I don't come back this way tomorrow because it's boring.

A school announced itself as the Holy Trinity Church of England Academy. This is really backing all the horses: Catholic, Protestant and corrupt government privatisation. Well, if GCSE results are bad they can always blame each other.

On Radio 5 this morning was an interview with a music therapist called Alison Hornblower. Can this be true?

I spent last week at the Cromer tennis tournament with, among others, Kelly, Gulam and Marvin. I wrote a piece about it, beginning as follows:

THE COMBINED AGES OF THE FOUR PLAYERS WAS 302.

THINK ABOUT IT...

CROMER NEVER CHANGES. THE CLUBHOUSE IS THE SAME. THE SUPERB COURTS ARE THE SAME. THE CAKES ARE THE SAME (WELL, NOT THE SAME CAKES AS LAST YEAR BUT SIMILAR). THE REFEREE AND ASSISTANTS ARE THE SAME, NEVER A DAY OLDER. FINALLY THE PLAYERS ARE THE SAME. IN FACT SOME OF THEM HAVE BEEN THE SAME SINCE THE 1950s.

'YOU REMEMBER OLD WHATSISNAME, WON HERE IN 1962, WHATEVER HAPPENED TO HIM?' 'OH, HE'S GONE.' 'AND THAT FELLA WITH THE GAMMY LEG, HE'S GONE TOO?' 'HOW HAVE YOU BEEN SINCE YOUR OPERATION? ONE NEW KNEE OR TWO? THREE? REALLY?' 'DID YOU HEAR WHAT HAPPENED TO OLD WHOSIT IN ALGECIRAS? THEY SAY THE WOMAN WAS NEVER THE SAME AGAIN...' 'WELL, I SUPPOSE WE'D BETTER GET ON AND PLAY. COULD YOU KEEP THE TEA WARM PLEASE, DEAR?'

Perhaps surprisingly, the club put it in its newsletter.

Day 83: Calne to Swindon (outskirts)
(18 August)

It was a day to make progress. It was unfortunate then that I set off in totally the wrong direction and had to walk all the way round Calne to get back on track. Thereafter it was uncontentious. Main roads led to minor roads. No climbs, no descents, no shops, no pubs, no problems.

Swindon lay ahead. Wasn't this supposed to be Britain's most affluent town a few years ago? I would never know. The road grew busier and busier and my route goes north from here, so I curved away without entering the town centre. It seems like a big place.

In less than a couple of weeks I take the train to Turkey and Georgia to watch a football match. I hope to fit in a couple of days' walking before I go. It's been a very long slog from Cornwall with no Qs at all until Queen Charlton, but from here they seem to come thick and fast. I hope to have a good time.

When I got back home to the village I told my friend Colin about the cat and the woodpecker. 'I hate cats,' he said.

Place name of the day: Interface. Can this be real? It's on a signpost.

Day 84: Swindon to Cricklade
(26 August)

The Great Flood has swamped the country. Again. Torrential rain has swept from west to east. Fortunately for me, the wind had accompanied it from left to right, so it was behind me, and the storm had gone off to East Anglia.

Apparently Swindon boasts the Magic Roundabout, the most complicated set of interchanges in the country. Apart from that, Swindon did not excite.

My friend Vicky lives nearby and joined me for a few hours. Eventually we found our way out of Swindon, entered a park and came out the other end in more or less the right direction for the canal to Cricklade. Not finding the canal was due to it having been filled in some years ago.

Outside Cricklade, a woman stopped her car to assist us in finding the footpath. 'Hop in,' she said kindly, not realising that this would totally undermine my project. 'It's on our land.' There was no denying her so we hopped in. Fortunately the point where she dropped us off was further from Cricklade than where she picked us up so the project was not undermined. The path was good too. The woman and her partner have eight hundred acres of dairy farm. Having sold their previous home they have been rehabilitating this land and are about to move in.

Vicky went home and I had a wander round Cricklade. Its picturesque main street has three pubs, a town hall, a library, a bank and NO CHARITY SHOPS. It also boasts some ancient bits involving a town crier and an official ale taster.

A surprise lay in store: a sign pointed to the Thames Path. I had no idea it came up here. It lies in wait for tomorrow.

Day 85: Cricklade to Fairford
(27 August)

'Isolated' heavy showers, they said. Huh. Isolationism was US foreign policy between the wars, allegedly. It was probably as isolated as these showers. They were right about the heavy though.

The morning went all right, in fact better than all right. The Thames Path was pleasant and easy and only two other people were on it. No-one could get lost and it passed quickly. I came out at Castle Eaton.

As I consulted the map, a man called out: 'You can get a cup of tea in the village hall if you want! Down there a hundred yards. They're just closing.'

As I told him, it was too good an offer to refuse.

And a bun.

On Thursdays, the travelling post office opens in the village hall in Castle Eaton. To celebrate this visitation, the community gathers, drinks coffee and eats sandwiches. On this occasion, goodies left over from a function last night were also on offer. I imagined it was a fundraising exercise and offered money but was not allowed to pay. I asked the post office man if he was treated with the same hospitality in all the villages where he opened for the day. Well yes, he said, he was.

Another man was being teased because he was putting out so many chairs for the evening's parish meeting. There's a popular item on the agenda, he retorted. Broadband.

No doubt it would be packed.

Reluctantly I pushed on and passed RAF Fairford. A gaggle of plane spotters had parked their cars by the road. They must be very patient people, these plane spotters, because this appeared to be the air force station without planes. Zilch planes. They're probably off bombing wedding parties somewhere in the Middle East.

Taking a wrong turning, I walked down the main road to Fairford. The plan was to continue to Quenington and beyond. However, it was piddling down. I realised that if I walked to Quenington I would have to walk back to Fairford to get a bus home. As they say in military circles, sod that for a game of soldiers. I had a cup of tea and eventually caught a bus for Swindon.

Fairford was historic, with flags.

On the map, all around is water. It's the Cotswold Water Park or something. I had never heard of it and it is invisible from the road.

Day 86: Fairford to QUENINGTON
to Cirencester
(10 October)

This has been the biggest ever gap between walks since I started this venture two and a half years ago. Why? Well, I went to Georgia to watch Scotland play football; and I went overland so it took a couple of weeks. Then I was ill and then I had to work. Feeble excuses, I know. I really must get on with it. I've said that before.

I sent the *Eastern Daily Press* intermittent reports from my trip. They printed a short piece about me before I went but showed regrettable lack of enthusiasm for the reports. So here they are!

Paris Saturday.

Paris was scorching. On the Eurostar I sat next to a nice young woman from Belfort, one of 300,000 French people currently working in London. She said London was better to work in because Paris is noisy and aggressive. I told her that where I come from London is seen the same way.

My usual treat in Paris is a pancake on the street but I couldn't find one. I spotted Naturalia. Is that a nudism shop or organic foods? It was the latter. I bought some goat's cheese and ate it all.

Saturday night and Sunday morning.

It never became absolutely clear what happened at Ulm but it was 'completely geschlossen'. Heat, points failures, twisted rails and electricity were in there somewhere. They shunted us into a little station at Stossen, handed out drinks and let us all play on the platform. Everyone was remarkably sanguine about it all. One might say it was the Dunkirk spirit if that wasn't completely inappropriate.

After two and a half hours we were off. I made the connection in Munich.

My companions in the overnight sleeper were already there. Where was I allocated? On the top, of course, just under the ceiling, with not quite enough length to contain my body and with just enough space above to break my nose if I sat up suddenly.

The big burly character in the compartment was going home after a Bayern Munich game. It would have been undiplomatic to mention Norwich's win there in 1993. The other character was an American working in 'contracts'. As soon as they say something like this you become suspicious. Was it computer contracts, building contracts? No, it was 'defence' contracts as I thought.

Budapest Sunday.

We spent seven hours talking!

George and Clarissa, Norwich City season ticket holders, are visiting friends in Budapest and doing a bit of work here. George, poet and translator, could talk for England. Clarissa isn't far behind. Nor am I. We had a wonderful day in which they took me to the most famous, ornate, gilded cafés in Budapest, each one more magnificent than the last. For respite we snacked in a hummus café.

They left me at the station in good time for the overnight, 22-hour train to Sofia.

Very good time.

Outside the station, a thousand poor Syrian refugees were demonstrating against their situation.

The notice board said the train was 30 minutes late. Then 50 minutes. Then 60. Then 90.

I made a new friend. Anna, a musician and voice over expert from Berlin, was heading to Istanbul to meet her husband, Greg. I thought she was about 26 until she told me she had a 28-year-old son.

Suddenly, after 180 minutes, several people with badges came bustling round the corner. The train on platform 6 was leaving! A small group of us dashed on board, thinking ourselves lucky. Then the train went round the corner and picked up everyone else.

The conductor, discovering that Anna was Russian by birth, gave us the best of everything. We had a choice of compartment: either air (the window worked) or light (it didn't work in that compartment). We chose air. It was 40 degrees on that train.

Romania Monday.

Light dawned over the beautiful Carpathians in Transylvania, which Howard and I drove through in his minivan 46 years ago. They were all dirt roads then.

At least I think it was the Carpathians. The light dawned on something anyway

We crossed the Romanian plain, then the Bulgarian plain, then the Bulgarian hills, then the Bulgarian mountains (very pretty), all the while two hours late, the conductor assuring us he had arranged for our connection to wait. Fortunately we didn't believe him or we might have been very disappointed. We arrived at least 90 minutes after our train had left. Stuck in Sofia.

Istanbul Tuesday.

Well, we got here.

By this time we were joined by Cyntia, Brazilian tour guide and traveller, who had missed a connection of her own in Sofia and was the only other passenger travelling through to Istanbul. We walked outside Sofia station and there was the bus station with a plethora of night buses to Istanbul. We chose the one with the world's grumpiest, nastiest, angriest conductor.

At the Turkish border I was singled out by the authorities. Why me? I was the only one who had to buy a visa. What has my country done to them? Something awful I expect.

We reached Istanbul several hours ahead of the train we had missed. After three overnights I shall sleep in a bed and do my washing.

The last time I came to Istanbul I walked here from Hook of Holland. This journey was definitely quicker than that.

Q

There would be little point in visiting Istanbul without eating baklava. It was Cyntia's birthday. We all ate at a famous baklava restaurant and she gave me a present. Greg talked about music and promised to send me some. Anna continued to organise everyone. Cyntia will go home as soon as she can get a flight.

Next day I caught the bus to Tbilisi. This is not as easy as it sounds and involved panic, frustration and a hair-raising taxi ride looking for the bus station.

Istanbul is a throbbing, thronging tourist town. Then, for fifty miles around, an extraordinary transformation has taken place. Huge building projects have changed the landscape beyond recognition. Villages have disappeared and in their place are vast housing complexes, hotels, businesses and workplaces.

Then the bus penetrates the rest of Turkey: fertile bits, arid bits, town and country and the Black Sea.

The journey to Tbilisi takes 27 hours. In our bus there was only one major snorer, a really good outcome in a packed bus of 50 or more. However, where was he sitting?

Yes, you guessed it.

Q

Tbilisi

At the border, first you get out of the bus and get checked by Turkish immigration. Then you do it all again for Georgian immigration. Then you get your luggage from the bus and go through Georgian customs. Then you wait an hour for the bus to do the same.

All sense of urgency seemed to have gone. We kept stopping for tea and cigarettes. It was time well spent though. Despite the heat, most places were bloomingly green. Slopes, hills and mountains were covered in trees. Plains and swamps bulged with fruit and veg.

Tbilisi arrived.

Later by arrangement I met the excellent Russell Martin, playing for Scotland, who had not one but two tickets for me for the match. He told me all the transfer news, which I knew nothing of, and we talked of books and babies and travel.

The match should be a stormer.

Q

Some travel tips for the Balkans.

1. It is almost impossible to remember that in Bulgaria a nod means no and a shake of the head means yes. Practise before you leave home. (Worth remembering too that the Greek word for yes is everyone else's word for no,)

2. You can charge your electrical equipment on the train but only when it goes fast enough. Wait for it to get up speed then get in there.

3. Washing your feet on the train is complicated when the only source of water is the tap that is worked by the foot pedal. You think you can do it? Try this at home too.

4, Don't be put off when, on entering Romania, your phone welcomes you to Serbia.

Q

Scotland lost the match and I am back on the Qs.

A kindly man came up and volunteered the best way to walk to Quenington, through the Oxpens and beside the river. This contrasted with a testy woman with dogs when I checked it out at the Oxpens. 'Well, Quenington is up that way somewhere but it's not the obvious or most direct way to go. Haven't you got a map or a compass?' It was in fact a pleasant walk and certainly the most obvious and direct way to go. Maybe she'd had a bad day.

Quenington seemed a pleasant and prosperous little place with a big village green. I didn't meet anyone and still haven't found out what it's like living in a place beginning with Q. To judge by Quenington, it's quiet.

The Romans went from here to Cirencester and they built

themselves a road to assist their journey. Today it was covered in cyclists, all of whom said hello to me. Things are looking up.

Cirencester looked cosy and is apparently steeped in history.

Place name of the day: Ready Token. Runner up: Ampney Crucis. My aunt and uncle Anne and David lived there latterly and I have been to some tragic funerals there.

Day 87: Cirencester to Stroud
(11 October)

Today I struck lucky. From the historic end of Cirencester lies a magnificent parkland, part of an enormous estate, with wide avenues leading back to the massive church. It was fine Sunday morning walking and I probably should have stayed on it, but after a while I returned to the main road for orientation, then zigzagged to picturesque Sapperton and Chalfont. Very good local advice pointed to the closed canal that led all the way to Stroud. With all the detours it was probably sixteen miles and it took six hours.

I used to average 3.5 miles per hour including stops. Then it was 3.5 mph without stops. Then it was 3 mph. Now it's 2.5 mph including stops. Soon it will probably be 2.5 without...

Anyway it was a lovely day for a walk and it was a lovely walk and very easy. Nice place.

I am reading *Fifty Shades of Grey* and a biography of Brian Lara. Let's hope I don't get them confused.

My boots have excellent new heels from the cobbler in Swaffham, with the effect that I scrape them along the ground all the time. My rucksack, after at least twenty years, is falling apart.

Day 88: Stroud to QUEDGELEY
to Gloucester
(28 October)

The world's most helpful tourist information officer works in Stroud. She more or less told me where to place my feet all the way to Gloucester. I still got lost. (The world's least helpful tourist information office works in Trieste. Beautiful city, pity about her.)

Whitehill, as you may guess, lies up a hill. It is a big hill and, after Whitehill, it gets even bigger. It was a glorious autumn day and, from the top, views lay over the Severn to the Forest of Dean; and indeed in all directions.

Over the top, a postman stopped his van. You can't possibly be delivering up here, I said. No, he was just sorting out his paperwork and computer tasks. When he started his job, he said, he had answered an advertisement for people with the social skills to help little old ladies. Now they'd be lucky to get a good morning. We discussed trade unions, renationalisation and all the other things chaps talk about when they get together. Then he remembered how busy he was and zoomed off.

Back at sea level, motorways and major roads cut across the land. Beyond them lay Quedgeley. I have seen worse. On the other hand, it was nothing to write home about. But that's another one of the little buggers ticked off. Arrivederci Quedgeley.

The city of Gloucester, on the other hand, has a good reputation which it largely lives up to. Last time I was here, for some work, I stayed in the Station Hotel. This time I splashed out elsewhere for £1 more. It wasn't worth it.

Day 89: Keynsham to Bath
(29 October)

It had not been forgotten that further back I had skipped a bit: namely Keynsham (spelled KEY...) to Bath. From Gloucester I go north, so this was my last real opportunity to fill it in. I arranged to meet my friend Liz and her dog Ted, who live in Bristol.

Liz and Nigel and I used to go walking in Switzerland with Andreas or on our own. Liz was phenomenally fit and ruthlessly left everyone behind. Then on a long descent she did her knee in and sadly it has never been the same since.

However, she can walk on the flat and we set out confidently. What neither she nor I could do, though, was read a map. You would think that walking straight up a valley, following road, railway and river, it would be impossible to get lost. We managed to find ourselves walking towards Bristol rather than Bath and on the wrong side of the river so that we had to clamber up a wood to get out.

But it gave us more time to reminisce. Trade unions, conferences, people we had known, walking, books, all the rest of it. We first met thirty-six years ago and worked together for a long while in the union (she was a lot fiercer than I was) but we hadn't had a proper talk for several years. We made up for it.

Bath is always nice to walk into and always crowded. Eschewing the tourist attractions today, we made our way to the station. She went to one side, I went to the other.

Day 90: Gloucester to Tewkesbury
(11 December)

This week it's a bad back and a stomach upset. For the last six weeks it's been a racking cough. None of that, however, explains why I haven't been walking since October. Even yesterday I had planned to go but it was raining buckets and I just couldn't be bothered. That's just moral turpitude.

I saw more of historic Gloucester than I intended. No-one anywhere had heard of the Severn Way which would lead me to Tewkesbury, and I wasted an hour looking for it. However, entertainment was laid on as a chap was apprehended on the main shopping street by the police. At least I hope it was the police: four of them in plain clothes. The chap really didn't want to go with them and he told them so. They formed a different view and didn't enter a debate on the matter.

From the docks I eventually found the Severn Way but a few minutes out of town it was blocked irretrievably. A Scottish woman whose dog was being attacked said it all happened with the major floods a few years ago. So it was back to the roads.

The A38 had a paved footpath. How far would it last? To the edge of town? To the nearest village? I kept looking to the next corner - and the one after - and the one after that. It couldn't go all the way, could it? But it did. Ten miles it went, all the way to Tewkesbury. It was not so much a walk, more a desperate trudge.

Not much appears to happen in historic Tewkesbury except for history. After five o'clock everybody leaves. Waiting for a bus was a young medical student called Alex, trying to get to Bristol. We sorted out the NHS, rugby, cricket, his shoulder injury and the tennis match at Wimbledon which, remarkably, both of us had been present at: Isner versus Mahut, the longest ever match. We didn't get on to discuss books because he didn't read anything ever. Apart from this he was a good chap.

Day 91: Tewkesbury to QUEENHILL to Upton upon Severn
(19 December)

Warm, wet, wild and woolly.

The friendly tourist office in Tewkesbury got out the maps and advised on routes to Queenhill, even though this involved crossing the border into Wales. The most important piece of advice was: don't take the Severn Way. The Severn had fallen by a metre overnight, but this begged the question of how many metres it was up in the first place. Ten metres up and then one metre down was still nine metres up. Best avoided.

Still, it was all going according to plan along a straightforward byway to Queenhill. The map, however, was at odds with reality. The byway was a Private Road. It said so in big letters. Some poxy school and private estate controlled it.

Instead I set off on a network of byways and paths which looked like plain sailing. We know what happened next. Slipping and sliding down on to a tarmac road I came across a village sign which was supposed to say Queenhill. Instead it said Longdon (no, not London), which was a very different kettle of fish and miles from where I wanted to be.

Eventually the elusive Queenhill revealed itself. According to the stats in the tourist office it has 170 residents. They must be very crowded in the half dozen houses I saw. Mind you, Queenhill Manor alone could take thirty.

Allegedly Elgar composed most of his music at Queenhill. I didn't hear him tonight though.

Upton upon Severn wasn't nearly as far as I had hoped to reach tonight.

Day 92: Pershore to Worcester
(8 January)

Yes, I know I finished last time at Upton upon Severn (really difficult to say Upton Upon) and I fully intended to go back there; the plan was to take the train to Pershore and catch the bus from there. But the only bus to Upton Upon went via Worcester, involved a change and took several hours. It would be dark before I arrived - if I arrived - and I would be very bad tempered. Meanwhile the distance from Pershore to Worcester was the same as from Upton Upon to Worcester, so we could pretend I was walking from Upton Upon. Admittedly this was untrue but was it cheating?

Two years ago, England was flooded. Two years later, from south-west England to northern Scotland it is flooded again. Cumbria, Lancashire, Leek, York, Aberdeen, all have been devastated. What has the government done to protect the country? According to them, they have put extra resources into flood protection. They are, however, lying. They have cut flood protection along with everything else. So the country has been flooded.

Footpaths, needless to say, were quagmires today, best avoided. Only once did I think about it and that led to getting lost in a mud heap. In Pershore, where the tourist office doubles as the library (another cut), the staff found a useful cycle map. Unfortunately I couldn't understand it so I returned once more to the indisputable Ordnance Survey. It's not their fault if footpaths disappear into thin air.

At home I have a shelf full of OS maps from the areas I have already covered. Apparently the market in second hand OS maps is booming so I shall donate them to Claire in Ceres Bookshop in Swaffham, doing her a favour and clearing space for me.

Perhaps I shall also sell my Wisden cricket almanacs to make space. But perhaps not.

I arrived in Worcester through a wide semi-circle of housing estates, in effect a whole new town. The city centre is old, with Friar Street the nub of the historic bit. The cathedral looms large; behind it lies the (usually flooded) cricket ground where visiting touring teams used to start their season. I didn't go round either.

I wrote a letter to my friend Andreas in Switzerland. For some time I have been urging him to walk round all the places in Switzerland beginning with the letter Z. It is a wonderful collection, starting in Zurich and encompassing Zermatt, Zernez, Zweissimen and Zofingen and many others. Initially enthusiastic, Andreas' ardour for the project seems to have waned. I hope I don't have to go and do it myself.

Day 93: Worcester to Bromsgrove
(27 January)

'If I get married now,' said the young woman across the aisle, 'I can get divorced at the end of July.'

The aisle of the train, that is, not the aisle of a church.

Behind her, another young woman was applying her underarm deodorant to the outside of her top. Does it work its way through to the armpit? There is so much to learn.

Meanwhile, after all this time I had a Companion again! Why suddenly so supportive? 'Well, I wouldn't mind doing that bit myself,' she said on looking at the congenial stroll along the canal from Worcester to Bromsgrove. So never mind the hard yards, it's fair weather walking only. (Mind you, last week we walked a killer from Whaley Bridge to Buxton in the snow. She doesn't mind punishment, for some reason she just doesn't like boredom.)

We toddled along the canal for sixteen miles. It was easy, pleasant and interesting until, quite suddenly, it became tiring, dour and tedious. All canals are like that but you can't really complain about an endless vista of ducks, moorhens, herons, boats and marinas.

Pubs dotted the route and we entered one for a cup of tea. Unfortunately I was so badly affected by the choice of music as we came in that I asked the barmaid if she was responsible. Perhaps I was a little abrasive on the matter but country music has that effect on me. Perhaps, too, I was a little demanding when we were only spending £2.80 on two teas and a packet of crisps and it was 3.30 in the afternoon with no other customers. Apart from its choice of music, The Bridge was a nice pub.

Bromsgrove might be a lovely town or may be a hell hole. We entered town near the station and saw nothing except the inside of a fantastic café-restaurant where the excellent food was quick, cheap and convivial. If all of Bromsgrove is like this, it's the place to be.

Day 94: Bromsgrove to QUINTON
(29 February - leap year - no offers)

The other day I spent £169 on pills. That's health pills, not even mentioning prescribed medication. I may be going on a specialised Parkinson's gluten free diet: no gluten, no carbohydrates but plenty of pills. My Companion took me to a health shop. 'This will cost you,' she said. She was right.

It's three years ago that I started this venture (the walk not the pills) on a snowy day in Norfolk. This is ridiculous. Dilatory, procrastinating, prevaricating, turpitudinous, all of them and more. I must get on with it.

Bromsgrove seemed all right. The diet hasn't started yet, which was good because I really like Greggs' cheese and onion quiches (hard to find - not in all stores). Later I was compelled by their advertising to stop in a garden centre. What were they recommending as a gift for Mothering Sunday? A garden shed (she could cook the tea there).

I was looking for Monarch's Way, which I haven't been on since Somerset or somewhere. I still haven't been on it because I couldn't find it. Through countryside enveloped in motorways I pushed on to Frankley. (As in the most famous line in cinema: 'Frankly, my dear, I don't give a damn.')

Strictly, I didn't reach Quinton. The road sign said it was a quarter of a mile away. I may have been still in Halesowen. However, I wanted to catch a bus to Birmingham and I will come back and do the necessary next time. Today I could see nothing remarkable in Quinton. Maybe that's because I was still a quarter of a mile short.

Place name of the day: Lickey End. Runner up: Frankley.

Day 95: QUINTON to QUARRY BANK to Wollaston
(no date in notebook)

I woke up the other day with a cut across my forehead. I knew nothing about it. What happened in the night? Did I head butt the headboard? It was a mystery. But I didn't look very good.

This was not helped by having new walking trousers, bought yesterday as a Christmas present (we celebrate Christmas in March round our way). They are excellent walking trousers. Only when I put them on today, however, did I realise that I should have bought a belt as well. I spent the day suffering from LCS (Low Crotch Syndrome).

Finally I have a heavy cold and keep coughing and spluttering everywhere.

I must have looked pathetic because people kept offering assistance. In Birmingham, eventually locating the number 9 bus for Quinton, the staff in Greggs showed endless patience as I dropped my money and asked directions. Outside, a man showed me the bus stop. Another man, who spoke no English, conveyed that my bootlaces were undone. Through my spluttering I thanked them all profusely. Then I caught the bus.

I can't think of anything to say about Quinton. It was there. That was it.

But there were two Qs in a day!

The Monarch's Way finally popped up for half an hour but the rest of the day was suburban. It was a relief when Quarry Bank appeared on a sign post since I was lost for most of the time. What was it like? Well, it was good to see that the Conservative Club looked more impoverished than the Labour Club. There was plenty of impoverishment. For once there weren't any charity shops on the main street, presumably because people couldn't afford to give anything away. It was mostly takeaways and doctors.

Oh, and there was a wool shop. My grandmother and then my aunts kept a wool shop in Manchester. People came from fifty miles around to ask advice about knitting or embroidery. My aunts spent their evenings knitting garments for their customers. And never charged for their labour.

On the subject of wool, Wollaston is, of course, pronounced Woolaston. As in: 'Is this the way to Wollaston?' 'Where?' 'Wollaston.' Blank faces. Then: 'Oh you mean Woolaston!'

In the pub an elderly guitar band played elderly songs - Willie Nelson, JJ Cale, the Everly Brothers. The place was packed with grey hairs, stomping.

Day 96: Wollaston to Alveley
(still no date)

When they make rude bus driving an Olympic event, he will certainly be on the podium. I was honoured to make the acquaintance of a future medal winner, outside Alveley, when he was running thirty minutes late and I was too tired to move fast. He was a corker.

The idea was to reach Quatt today, making three Qs in two days. But the bus timetable was hazardous so I decided to take the early bus (thirty minutes late) back from Alveley and call it a day.

The passers-by entertained me during the waiting-for-the-bus interval. 'Oh, they come when they feel like it.' 'Sometimes they don't come at all.' 'Oh, that's nothing...' The passers-by were very friendly. Unlike the driver.

Wollaston is on the very edge of the Birmingham complex. (That sounds like an illness.) From there, past a couple of stately homes, lies the country. Apparently they intend to make the whole area into a garden city. They should call it Oxymoron.

It was further and harder than I thought. Kinver, down a bloody great hill (meaning you have to go up a bloody great hill on the other side) was picturesque. I asked the way of a fresh faced young PCSO. She had never heard of Alveley, which was at least three miles away as the crow flies, but she got out all her machinery and directed me definitively to the north. It wasn't the way I had planned but I didn't have the heart to reject her so I walked the extra mile or so. Spectacular sandstone houses drew the crowds even in March.

Rolling farmland led to Alveley and the bus led to Kidderminster. I used to know someone called Kidderminster, Michael Johnson's client. He was rather lively.

Day 97: Alveley to QUATT to QUATFORD to Bridgnorth
(date unknown)

Well, what a good/bad day. Either it's an extravagant disaster or it's the opportunity to re-think the whole next stage. Shropshire is big, bold and awkward. How do I get to Quabbs?

First, though, I take it all back. Shropshire bus drivers today were the politest, classiest, most helpful bunch in the world. And as for the passengers! A man in Kidderminster who had retired after fifty years' work in only two jobs told me every detail of the two alternative routes to Bridgnorth, one of them mine. Another man was going for a job interview in electrical engineering, in which he had a PhD and had been lecturing in east London. He had progressed to the second interview stage so he was hopeful.

Alveley, like everywhere else, used to have a shop and a post office but now seems like a dormitory town. The only way forward from here was the main road, a slow and tedious experience as I spent most of the time on the bank. But soon came Quatt. On the map it seems like the blink of an eye. In reality, yes, it goes in the blink of an eye, a clutch of nice houses and apparently a vibrant bell ringing group. Then it was on to Quatford, which has a National Trust property and a castle! The River Severn came close and went away again. I should be looking round these places. But Bridgnorth lay ahead.

Outside town, two old ladies (my age) said there was no such thing as a town centre in Bridgnorth, only a High Town and a Low Town. I climbed up to High Town. This is like a French town, on top of a big hill. It's also rather old and splendid, quiet and traditional, full of Tudor whatsits.

The plan was to walk another four miles to Morville, where my friend Cathie was due to share a cup (or two cups) of tea with me and then drive me back to Bridgnorth. However, by this time it was far too late to meet her so I had to be content with Bridgnorth even though it was only a miserable eight miles for the day. Tomorrow I have to be at the sad funeral of a young person in Warrington.

How to spend an evening in Bridgnorth? I went to the cinema. No-one else did. I was the only person in the cinema. Admittedly the film wasn't very good.

I shall take advice on walking across Shropshire to whatever that place is called on the other side, miles and miles away.

Day 98: Bridgnorth to Burwarton
(6 July)

It's too boring to go into detail about my absence. In summary, the heart went wrong for the first time in six years. The doc listed me for the normal process: see the heart man with a view to either a cardioversion (electric shock) or an ablation. But then my Companion took charge.

She put me on a combination of taurine and L-arginine, a (legal) favourite of body builders. It didn't build up my body (you still have to do the work for that apparently, not just sit in a chair and watch) but it sorted out the heart overnight. No procedure needed.

But meanwhile the heart problem had a bad effect on the Parkinson's. We're working on that one.

So it was a few weeks before we got it all under control and then I built up some confidence and finally a notion of fitness. After the hiatus I was back again in Bridgnorth. Actually I was convinced that I had walked further than Bridgnorth; I could even picture it. But the notebook does not lie. I had imagined greater progress than I had actually made. It could be an illustration of my life.

Shropshire is green and verdant and above all it's hilly. Which is what the eighty-seven-year-old cyclist said when we compared maps at a junction. It's hilly. In fact he said that when you got to eighty you needed some assistance so he had a motor fitted to his cycle. Then it wasn't so hilly.

'GIVE WAY 335 YARDS,' said the sign. What? Why? It's like the signs in West Norfolk that say 'GIVE WAY 142 YARDS.' No-one has ever been able to explain it and the same applies here. Why 335?

I took the road called Jed Mytton Way, which was closed to traffic. I don't know who Jed Mytton was (or is - shouldn't jump to conclusions, sorry mate) but his silent road would have earned the respect of many a walker. Cleobury North was an opulent collection of stone homes, rather beautiful. By the time I reached Burwarton I was barely moving.

Day 99: Burwarton to Ludlow
(7 July)

I unearthed some poems I wrote a long time ago. It's all right, they're not going in here. One of them might pass muster as a light hearted romp. If it seems halfway presentable I will put it in somewhere, maybe at the end. If it's not there, wiser counsel prevailed.

I'm getting to grips with the logistics of Shropshire. In essence, I can't do anything I had planned. I was going to pop over to Craven Arms from Burwarton, but the slightest look at a proper map shows a whole load of contour lines close together. That means no. Then the two highest hills in Shropshire (allegedly) lie either side of the main road to Ludlow. That means no diversions. I always wanted to see Ludlow anyway.

'I'm totally lost!' So cried the motorist who stopped opposite me, trying to reach her sister in Cleobury Mortimer but led astray by traffic diversions. She might count herself fortunate to come across a man walking down the main road with a map open in his hand. For my part, I now know how to pronounce Cleobury. Clibbery.

No contest for place name of the day then.

Ludlow is full of hills but apart from that it's very nice. The lady in the bookshop had never heard of Quabbs, my far off destination, and nor has anyone else; but we searched the maps to find the right one to buy.

That's the first hundred days then. If I can just deal with Shropshire, maybe it will fall into place.

Day 100: Ludlow to Bucknell
(26 July)

It was a bit of a day.

I wouldn't blame the excellent people in the bookshop in Ludlow, who gave super directions; when I looked back on the day I even remembered the bit about having to cross a few fields. The main problem was it was just too bloody far. Certainly that's what the police thought.

For a long time the path went through pleasant woodland, but then for no accountable reason it went steeply uphill. What was up there? Nothing really. Then came the bit with the fields and a lot of sheep, leading down to a stately home called Downton (yes) Castle. Eventually Downton Gorge led to Downton Rock and it was clear I wasn't going to catch the train to Bucknell to stay the night.

I tried.

And I failed. By an hour, which is quite a long time to miss a train by.

At Leintwardine I considered my options. It was eight o'clock and there weren't any options really. I set off to try to walk it and then everything changed.

At the edge of the village three police vehicles had been dealing with a minor incident. I made an enquiry of a constable about time and distance and the sergeant overheard. 'Don't bother with that,' he said. 'My colleague will take you.'

That was very kind though counter-productive for my purposes. But then, of course, before I was allowed in the car they had to do a full check. Name, address, date of birth. When he heard my date of birth the sergeant's head shot up as if he had been stung. Elderly gents from Norfolk should certainly not be wandering round Shropshire at that time of night. His colleague was to take me anywhere I needed to go, even though it was out of area and breaching policy. Anything else?

In fact we had an interesting trip. The officer detailed to take me lived with his partner and children in Ludlow, which had been his home all his life. He was prepared to go not only out of county but out of country (into Wales) to get me safely indoors. In return I was able to give him some tips about dyslexia which might even change his life. It would be rude, considering his kindness, to talk about his sense of direction.

Earlier a weasel ran backwards and forwards across the road. Half a mile further on, two young blackbirds sat immobile on the tarmac. Their mother hopped up and down making a lot of noise and then flying a few feet further, hoping to distract me away from the chicks. I hoped the weasel didn't come any further up the road or their lives would be over in seconds.

Day 101: Bucknell to Knucklas
(27 July)

Next day, of course, I had to go back and walk the route I had covered by police car last night. I hoped none of the police spotted me. Walking down the same road from Bucknell station, they might have thought I was taking the piss. All was quiet, however, and I slid quickly out of the village.

Knighton is the jumping off point for Offa's Dyke. Looking at the map, it would be the shortest way for me to reach my destination. Looking more carefully at the map, however, NAH! NOT BLOODY LIKELY! Those contour lines, there are thousands of them and they're unbelievably close together. Nah, that's for hard people.

I took the road back to Knucklas in plenty of time for my train out. A Tesco delivery van pulled up, the driver insistent that he must give me a lift for the three-quarters of a mile to the turn off. I couldn't tell him I didn't want a lift, any more than I could tell him how much I hated Tesco and didn't want to be seen climbing out of his van. Eventually I gave in; that meant I was half an hour early for the train.

It turned out that the driver was himself a very experienced walker and always stopped for other walkers when it was hot or wet (which it was neither). We had a good chat for three-quarters of a mile.

While waiting for the train, entertainment was provided by half a dozen young teenage girls, on their way to Knighton to share three curries between the six of them. (The police officer last night said there was an outstanding curry house in Knighton.) They were normal kids: funny, cheery, considerate and courteous. They were extremely polite to me. And incredibly foul mouthed among themselves.

Day 102: Knucklas to QUABBS to Newcastle (Salop)
(15 August)

Outside Knucklas, a man and a large rucksack emerged from a field.

'Where did you spring from?' I asked.

'From that field,' he said.

He was wearing a placard saying 'Glider - please assist.' I thought this must be some new terminology for begging and prepared to give him a quid. But he was trying to hitch a ride into town. He had glided into the field.

I asked what he had done with his glider. He said it was in his rucksack. This caused wild speculation on my part. With the best of intentions and modern skills, I still couldn't see how you could fold a plane into a rucksack. Then it dawned at last. He was a hang glider or para glider or one of those gliders. He had come from the Malvern Hills, forty miles away.

His record for distance was seventy-five miles. He pointed up high into the blue sky, where he said the second best glider in the country was making tracks. But it wasn't a good day today because there wasn't enough cloud. When there's cloud you can see the wind patterns and use them. My friend here had gone as far as he could, then spotted a town with a railway station and would try, with the aid of his placard, to make his way home again.

I crossed the river and took the scenic route: tiny lanes and no traffic but unfortunately plenty of hills. That's the trouble with scenic routes. Then there was the big climb, up to 1,300 feet with huge views over deep green valleys and rolling hills. These must be the Shropshire Hills.

And Quabbs.

Up at the top, a signpost had a little round bit at the top. 'Quabbs,' it said.

So I'm in the centre of Quabbs.

But isn't there something missing? Like the rest of Quabbs? Like houses? People? Where are they?

Maybe I passed a farm on the way in. I saw no other habitation. I've walked fifty miles round Shropshire looking for a place that isn't there. It's no wonder no-one had heard of it. It doesn't exist.

(I should qualify that statement. One person had heard of it: the incredibly self-possessed fourteen-year-old called Martha who served my meal in the evening and then sat down for a chat in preference to helping with the washing up. But she was the only one.)

Day 103: Newcastle (Salop) to Craven Arms
(16 August)

Oh, what an unholy cockup I made of today.

It was the poached eggs.

Everything was planned. Start walking at 8.00, catch the train at 13.00, make a set of connections and reach Norwich at 19.15, just before kickoff at the football at 19.45. A bit sweaty, perhaps, and carrying a rucksack but otherwise perfect. Simon would drop me at home afterwards.

They didn't start breakfast until 8.00.

Then the poached eggs took half an hour to come. I should have left without them. But I had paid for breakfast. More and more agitated, when they arrived I gobbled them. Too late.

I was too pissed off to finish this chapter.

Day 104: Craven Arms to Church Stretton
(7 September)

The Shropshire Way leads exactly from Craven Arms to Church Stretton. It is peaceful, secluded and beautiful.

Obviously I didn't go that way.

It goes on a wild detour and, worse, climbs a bloody great hill. It carries the almost certain guarantee of getting lost.

The last time I was at Craven Arms I was so pissed off that I might have been unfairly prejudiced. I thought it was a bit of a dump. Since then, people have told me that it was part of their walking holidays and that it has all sorts of cultural goodies. I came back to stay tonight, after walking to Church Stretton, because it seemed likely to be cheaper. And it was. Why? Because it's a bit of a dump.

The scenery, however, is another matter. What an extraordinary area this is. It ought to be in Scotland. Huge hills, covered in moorland, sweep down into deep wooded valleys; the entry into Church Stretton is spectacular. I have been here before, a decade or so ago with my friend Sheila who wanted to walk the Long Mynd after travelling on the wonderful train from London that had the best food and friendliest staff in the world. (It's gone now, of course.) We walked the Long Mynd and went home again. It's much too hard to do again now.

A community shop dispensed walking directions and the cheapest food in Shropshire. Shocked at how little I was spending there and wanting to support the shop, I kept buying more items. I eventually got the bill up to nearly £2. Then I set off on what was laughably called a bridleway.

The plan was to stay with Cathie and John tonight but Cathie is now so eminent in tennis circles that she is off to the Olympics and the US Open. So it's Craven Arms.

Day 105: Church Stretton to Shrewsbury
(8 September)

So it all turned out as planned then.

I wasn't sure if I could walk from Church Stretton to Shrewsbury in the five hours before my train left. But there were fool-proof safeguards. Either I could walk for four hours, catch the country bus and come back another time to finish it; or I could walk for four hours to the edge of town, catch one of the plentiful local buses and follow the same process.

The 435 bus arrived in Shrewsbury eleven minutes before the train left. The bus station was bound to be adjacent to the railway station and the bus was bound to be on time.

Hmmm.

The 435 was fifteen minutes late. As for the local buses, they took about four days to travel from the edge of town to the bus station - which was nowhere near the railway station. I was booked on a fixed train out of Shrewsbury so, having missed it, I had to buy a fresh ticket. It made me savage (as Norfolk would say).

The five hours' walking was easy enough. Four dogs chased me off a public footpath. The back roads were quiet.

From a distance two cyclists approached amid a monotone of conversation. It wasn't clear whether it was two men talking or one man and a very quiet woman. As they passed, their voices were revealed. All she said was 'really?' 'really?, 'really?' from time to time. It was all he needed: an audience.

Once on a train in south Germany I watched a middle-aged couple repeat their lifestyle. For several hours he talked, making a series of a statements. She said, *bitte?* Then he made the statement again. It drove me mad but didn't seem to bother them.

Day 106: Shrewsbury to Wem
(8 October)

Clive. Strange name for a village.

By sheer fluke I made all the right choices today, unlike all the other days. Then at the end I made a very bad choice.

First I took the A-road instead of the more direct B-road; it turned out to have a footpath for several miles and then came a real bridleway, hard and open and totally splattered with cattle dung. This led to Clive, which was strange in every way. It was invisible from the outside world. Cut off by a sudden collection of rock faces, it constituted a world of its own. It was stunning. I congratulated one of the inhabitants on the beauty of her village. She agreed.

But what a strange name. There were signs to Clive Church and Clive Hall, as if they were the names of residents. Apparently the name is a derivative of Cliffs rather than a commemoration of Clive of India, who lived not far away.

Place names of the day: 1. Clive. No contest; 2. Wem; 3. Honourable mention: Pankeymoor. Allegedly there is also a village called Sleep.

The road to Wem was long and straight, causing every young man in a car to want to assert his masculinity. They scared the shit out of me. If I'm going to be run down by a maniac I want it to be somewhere beginning with a Q not a W.

I reckoned there must be somewhere to stay in Wem. I was wrong. Everywhere was full. The question has to be asked: why would anyone want to stay in Wem? I don't want to be unkind but I could think of no reason why all the beds were full. Wem doesn't really have a lot going for it.

It didn't get any better. I sat at the bus stop for the bus back to Shrewsbury to find somewhere to sleep. The bus to Shrewsbury went off in the opposite direction. I just couldn't understand it. Eventually I caught a train, and would come back in the morning.

Shrewsbury was in human turmoil. Every young person in Shropshire was there, mostly in little black dresses. Most of the older people were here too, but they were coming later for the long haul. The town was shaking.

Day 107: Wem to QUINA BROOK to Prees
(9 October)

I had breakfast with Emma, an old friend whom I hadn't seen for at least twenty-five years. We had some catching up to do and an hour in which to do it before her Sunday morning conference call with her children. (The children are not still at home, I should point out.)

Emma has been the Green Party candidate in a couple of general elections. One day she will win.

Then the trains weren't running because of a fatality. They put us in a taxi to Wem.

In the taxi was a young woman going back to visit her parents after moving into town. Fluent in French and Spanish after living in both countries, she has just graduated and taken her first job with a vehicle tracking company. (As she said, there aren't many opportunities for French- and Spanish-speakers in Shropshire.) The company develops the new technology, like a souped up tachograph, showing not only the hours driven but also the exact location, so that if the driver goes off route by ten metres the company in Paris or Marseille or Lyon can be on the phone - or screen - in moments. Scary.

Why, I asked her, was Wem so full last night? She couldn't imagine. There is nothing, absolutely nothing, to do in Wem. But the people are friendly. Perhaps that's it. Perhaps the tourists just came to meet the friendly people.

Oh - nearly forgot – Quina Brook! Well, it would be easy to forget. Indeed it would be easy to miss it altogether. In a moment there it was - gone.

I have just realised there is a Q on the Isle of Man. I'm not going there. Mainland only.

Day 108: Prees to Loggerheads
(11 November)

I am at Loggerheads.

I have wanted to say that since I first saw the name.

It was a difficult day though. The road from Prees was uneventful as far as the junction, but walking along the A41 would have meant certain death. A detour led through the villages to the A53, which had a footpath all the way to Market Drayton.

A wonderful veggie breakfast at Rumbling Tummies stoked up the afternoon and I was ready to go. No-one, however, could answer the important question of the day. Was there a footpath beside the A53 to Loggerheads?

No-one working in Market Drayton appeared to live there. Everyone I asked commuted by car and neither knew nor, frankly, cared whether there was a footpath. However, the answer finally came with the wonderful woman from the library, who lives in Loggerheads. And the answer was no.

As far as the turning to Almington, she said, there was a path. Then she went through every possible combination of detours including walking through the woods at night. There wasn't any realistic route.

So I set off along the footpath as far as the turning to Almington. It came. The footpath carried on. And on. Ah, what does she know, thinking she knows the area...

There was a second turning to Almington.

I was a smarty pants. She was right. There was no footpath.

There was a grass bank which was slow, hard and tedious. Apart from that it was fine. A woman stopped her car, a brave but foolish thing to do on that road, to offer a lift through the narrow bit ahead. I declined, of course, but took the hint and made for the fields instead. They were slow, hard and tedious too and it was dark when I reached Loggerheads.

Tomorrow was planned for more walking but frankly the weather forecast talks of cold heavy wet rain. No thank you. None of that.

I took the bus and asked the driver if he went past a train station. 'I'll see what I can do,' he said. It seemed a strange answer in the circumstances.

Day 109: Loggerheads to Penkhull
(8 December)

Mick Gough made me sandwiches! He also gave me an apple, banana, tangerine, biscuits and water: a packed lunch for a mammoth. He met me at Stoke station and drove me to Loggerheads, pointing out all the roads with and without footpaths. Then he went home and I set off to walk back to Stoke.

In Ashley a plaintive notice asked people not to keep stealing the lights off the community Christmas tree. At Maer, a sign in a window stated that 'Elvis and Mrs Elvis slept here twice.' Can this be true?

Maer is a baronial hamlet. A bridge across the road leads from the baronial seat to the church. Apparently Charles Darwin had connections.

The A53 led all the way to the centre of Newcastle-under-Lyme and by that time it was dark. It stayed dark all the way to Penkhull.

Asking directions brings the following: 'Excuse me, is this the way to Penkhull?' Pause. Examination. Consideration. Then reply: 'Are you from round 'ere?'

Now, there are two things to say about this response. First, what difference does it make to the directions? Second, if I was from round here I wouldn't be needing directions. In fact, everyone is incredibly friendly and just about takes you home with them. But you have to get used to being called Duck.

Penkhull has apparently been here since the Domesday Book. It can seldom have provided such hospitality as given by

Mick and Nicki. After lavish nutrition they even followed the Kosovan code of hospitality: when you leave they give you a present to thank you for enabling them to give you hospitality: in this case a Portmeirion mug.

Until a late hour we reminisced. Mick told a tale of meeting someone, for work, off a flight from Ireland in the time of the Troubles. In the airport he turned round from making a phone call and discovered he was surrounded by Special Branch pointing guns at him. Staying very calm, he explained that he was meeting someone for work.

'I'm a probation officer,' he said.

'Oh, that's all right then sir.'

Those were the days.

Day 110: Penkhull to Cheadle (Staffs)
(9 December)

Mick made me another packed lunch. Nicki pursued me by car to give it to me. I set out on the long, long climb up to Werrington, then on the back roads to Cheadle. A pub stood beside a road called Westacre. It seemed an omen since I would be back in Westacre tonight so I had a cup of tea there. It was dark when I arrived in Cheadle.

A curiosity of my condition (PD) is that when I'm really tired I veer to the right. Outside Cheadle a very friendly and responsible local councillor (he told me he was a councillor) warned me I was swerving from the pavement too close to the traffic. In fact he ran after me to warn me again. Trying to reassure him, I said mildly (but foolishly): 'I am quite experienced.'

'You will be if you get run over,' he said.

To get home, I caught the bus from Cheadle to Uttoxeter. A train led from Uttoxeter to Derby. Another train led to Nottingham. Another train led to Ely, where my train to Downham Market was cancelled. When I eventually reached Downham my car had two parking tickets on it.

What! I had paid!

By the time I got home I could barely walk.

Day 111: Cheadle (Staffs) to QUIXHILL
to Rocester (not Rochester)
(3 January)

Well, I think that was Quixhill.

A new (and equally fantastic) speech therapist called Penny has given me some different catch phrases. Instead of 'That's not acceptable', 'No sugar' and 'A return to Dartford please' I now have to practise - topically – 'We wish you a merry Christmas', 'Not another pair of socks' and 'I really don't like mince pies.' Today's route involved a lot of tight bends and blind corners. After a while I stopped shouting out my new catchphrases and concentrated on minding the traffic. I would hate my last words to be 'Not another pair of socks.' Or, for that matter, 'We wish you a merry Christmas.' It's not exactly 'Kiss me, Hardy' (Nelson) or even 'Bugger Bognor' (George V).

Did I get to Quixhill? I think so.

It's a speck on the map, just outside Dunstone. I walked over the bridge and up the Ashbourne road. To the left stood some classical arches, leading presumably to a stately home. A couple of houses loomed. By now it was pitch dark and the attractions of Quixhill were waning fast. Was this it? Had I done it? Later my landlady said this was it. I had been there.

Rocester is pronounced Roester. It was a Roman village. It was a mill town. It is now home to JCB, the largest privately owned company in the country. I had not realised that JCB is so-named after its founder, Joseph Cyril Bamford. The HQ is vast but apparently all landscaped with lakes and suchlike.

In the chippy I had a quorn burger. Then in an establishment which shall be nameless I had the worst pint for a very long time.

What was that, away to the north? Ah, yes. Alton Towers. Where to have fun. But I didn't want any fun.

Day 112: Rocester to Mackworth
(4 January)

Winter is here.

'Not another postman in shorts,' I said.

'It's not too bad today,' he said. 'Warmer than yesterday.'

This was true. But it didn't mean it was above freezing.

A bit further on stood the Hungry Bentley barn. A woman was clipping a hedge and I asked her who Bentley was and why he was so hungry. Apparently the whole area was called Hungry Bentley. The land was so poor that it could not sustain the people living on it.

'Probably the same now,' I said.

An old Roman road ran across the map. I envisaged a spectacular flat ridge, dead straight, looking out over the whole country like the Hog's Back in Surrey. In fact it was largely low and boring and it wasn't even straight. And it certainly wasn't flat. As soon as possible I went back to the main road.

The next mission, from Mackworth to Quarndon, needs a man with a plan. I think I know just the man.

Day 113: Mackworth to QUARNDON to... well...
(12 January)

Oh no, not again!

The man with the plan was Jon.

We met at the station with some difficulty, since we were both wearing headgear and didn't recognise each other. He has also lost three stone to combat diabetes.

Jon and Heather gave me nourishing and excellent soup and then he and I went walking. There was much to discuss. Jon might be thought elderly; certainly he is old school polite and gentlemanly. When he retired from the Probation Service he founded a chamber music society in Derby which successfully promotes concerts. All this could veil Jon's views on life. He is very, very militant. He is militant about everything. He is militant about government cuts, he is militant about cars parking on the pavement, he is militant about bus travel, he is militant about poetry. He uses buses all the time and has a very personal attitude towards going walking in the Peak District. When he feels like a walk he goes to the end of the street. He waits for a bus. Whichever is the first bus, he takes it. Wherever it goes, he goes. He gets off there, walks for the day and comes home again. It saves time on planning.

Jon walked with me to Quarndon and showed me a house called The Quandary where his friend lives. I ought to get a bonus point for a house beginning with Q. His friend is a physicist, which Jon thought was suitable for a man living in The Quandary. We walked on, he showed me the byway for the next part of the route and then he turned for home.

Then the trouble started.

It was undeniably going dark. By the time I got to Brailsford it would have been dark for an hour. But it was only five o'clock. If it had been summer no-one would have dreamed of phoning the police...

Just to make sure I was going in the right direction, I had asked the way three times: a couple walking their dog, a young woman on a horse and a farmer. They all confirmed the route but seemed excessively concerned with how far it was at that time of day. One of them presumably rang the police. On a deserted stretch of lane where no vehicle at all had passed, a cruiser came to a halt beside me.

The most flattering part of it all was that the woman in charge simply would not believe my age. She kept asking me to repeat my date of birth. Unfortunately, the age then just made it worse. She was concerned that I must be mad or lost or both. I was, as I kept saying, by no means lost. In fact it was unprecedented: I knew exactly where I was. Whether I was mad or not was, of course, a matter of opinion.

She and her sidekick made calls. They discovered that back in Norfolk I was neither wanted nor certified. With my agreement they even rang my Companion. They asked if wandering around Derbyshire after dark was normal behaviour for me. On being told yes, it was quite normal behaviour for me, they all had a good chuckle at my expense. Women, eh.

The sergeant then said that because it was late at night – 'late at night!' I said, 'it's only five o'clock!' – well, after dark, they were concerned about my safety and wanted to drop me at the pub in Brailsford, just down the road. I didn't really have much choice. So we had a laugh and I told them I would be committing them to print and they asked me to say something nice about them and I promised I would. Then they dropped me in the pub car park.

Consternation broke out. Seeing a cop car in the car park was too much for a couple of customers called nosey and parker who dashed out to ask stupid questions. Within two minutes the story was going round the pub. 'Found him lost. Wandering round a field.'

The customers and staff were friendly, however. I asked quietly about buses to Ashbourne to find a bed for the night and it transpired that everyone in the pub had a bus timetable on them which they promptly whipped out. It reminded me of a hotel lounge in Chandigarh when the receptionist answered the phone. 'Telephone call for Mr Singh!' he announced. Twenty customers rose as one. Every man in the Punjab was Mr Singh.

The police took me about one and a half miles. Earlier in the day I missed half a mile or so round Allestree. I probably owe two miles. Say three to be on the safe side.

Day 114: Brailsford to Ashbourne.
Or rather...
(13 January)

Derbyshire woke to a coating of snow. Despite vowing never to do it again, I resorted to the last refuge. Instead of walking from Brailsford to Ashbourne I walked from Ashbourne to Brailsford. It was just so much easier.

Ashbourne golf course must surely be the country's hilliest. Whenever I use that word 'surely' I am reminded

of that wonderful line in *Airplane*: 'Don't call me Shirley!')
Almost immediately, however, a different hazard reminded me
of what I hadn't brought: sun glasses.

I had snow blindness in Switzerland once. It was
entirely my own fault; I had sun glasses in my pocket but
for some reason didn't use them. Staying in a mountain hut,
I lay down for the night, eyes streaming and almost totally
unseeing, and in the morning an elderly lady, one of the hut
wardens, took me by the hand and led me through a tunnel
to a cable car. There I rang Lilian and said I was coming to
stay for a few days. The first day I just lay down in the dark.
After about four days I could manage, but one eye is still
affected today.

After the golf course I found myself on Bonnie Prince
Charlie Way and then Osmaston Park which was very pretty.
After a few villages I took to the main road.

Apropos of nothing at all, several times this week I have
found myself telling my Vincent Price story. It has nothing to
do with the walk but it may be worth telling.

Fifty-one years ago the actor Vincent Price was filming a
horror movie (probably - a movie anyway) at Castleacre. One
day my father happened to be in the bar of The George at
Swaffham when the cast of the film came in. My father bought
a round.

Then - wait for it - Vincent Price stole his change!

Ever afterwards, when Vincent Price came on television,
my father cried out: 'He stole my change!'

Days 115-116: Ashbourne to Buxton
(20-21 January)

Quotes:
> 'Buxton'll be grand when it's finished.'
> 'No point having a bath without a good novel. Waste
> of water.'
> 'I wouldn't make long term plans for you and U3A if
> I were you.'

It is, of course, complete coincidence that my Companion happened to be free on exactly the day when I walked through some of the most beautiful countryside in England. She was unfortunately tied up during the whole of the hard slog previously.

I didn't buy any maps of the next bit because I already had some: fifty-five-year-old maps which must have been my father's. High quality and durable, they still showed railway lines that were closed down fifty years ago. Perfect.

We started with lunch. Ashbourne is a good place for that. Then what could be better than Dovedale? Following up river the path continues into Beresford Dale, which is just as beautiful; and we basically pursued the river all the way to Hartington.

Or should have done.

There are few people in the world with a worse sense of direction than me; but unfortunately I was walking with one of them. The same person will brook no argument when suddenly possessed of a notion to go around some lengthy and possibly fatal short cut. We climbed a small mountain and I, for one, was totally nick-knacked by the time we reached The Devonshire Arms in Hartington. It was dark too.

Next day was spellbinding. The mist rose, the sky was totally clear and we walked in more or less the right direction. On a day like this, nowhere in the world is better than the Peak District. Hartington itself is a picturesque village. A bit further on, stunning views led over the Manifold Valley, even more beautiful than Dovedale. A couple of miles before Buxton is the remarkable warehouse bookshop which you cannot walk past without stopping. When you add the amazing second hand bookshop in Buxton itself, this is a literary district.

We arrived at dusk.

I was born in Buxton. Admittedly I left at three weeks old to go to Norfolk but we frequently visited and learned all the dales, villages and walks in the area. We swam in the thermal baths, walked up to Solomon's Temple and saw The Who in the Pavilion Gardens in 1964 or 1965. We ate oat cakes and were stopped on the street by everyone, thirty or forty years after he left, who thought they hadn't seen my father for a while.

One day in Norfolk, working on the straw carting trailer, my workmate Cally Shackcloth said to me: 'Of course, you're not a Norfolk man.'

'Excuse me,' I said, 'but I have lived here all my life.' (Except for the three weeks.)

'Yes,' he said, 'but your parents weren't Norfolk people. Your children could be Norfolk people but you can never be a Norfolk man.'

It's true, of course. Even if I could have got there three weeks earlier, I could never be a Norfolk man. Perhaps I am a Derbyshire man.

There is no point in waxing lyrical at length about Dovedale and the Manifold Valley. It has all been done. They're great.

Days 117-118: Buxton to Bredbury
(2-3 February)

Whenever I walk with anyone else they seem to take charge. Can't think why but it suits me very well. Over two days David found a decent map, planned the route, carried the bag, made my sandwiches and gave good conversation. Oh, and he and Lynne put me up for the night.

Forty-two years ago I forgot to turn up for a game of tennis with David and he was left standing on the court. It is the only game of tennis I have ever forgotten and I have felt guilty ever since. There is no way of atonement. In fact, they give me more and more hospitality and I find myself ever deeper in their debt.

We walked from Buxton up the main road over Long Hill then down to Goyt Valley, where we used to play as children on holiday. You wouldn't play there now as it's under the Errwood Reservoir. My map was made before the reservoir was built so it looks still accessible. Over the dam we continued to the Fernilee Reservoir; my father used to walk here in the 1930s before this one was built. It's still a very pretty walk down the valley, ending at the beautiful hamlet of Taxall. We dribbled into Whaley Bridge, missed the train by thirty seconds because I was too tired to run, adjourned for a swift half and a packet of salt and vinegar then caught the next one.

It was a convivial evening - and morning - with talk of books, children, grandchildren and politics. I have known all the children since they were babies. Sophie and Rosie put in an appearance again today.

Bredbury was not part of the plan. However, at Whaley Bridge we had spotted a canal and, well, you know how I feel about canals. Who cared where it went? It went somewhere and it was flat.

Or, at least, for a while it was flat. Through New Mills it reached Marple, where a stunning feat of engineering transformed the journey and the landscape. Sixteen locks dropped the canal over two hundred feet; and a historic aqueduct led across the Goyt Gorge. At the moment the canal is drained in places for major repairs but it is still an amazing spectacle. It was a great day.

David and I have been walking together now for two whole days but we still seem to be on good terms. At least I think so.

Day 119: Bredbury to Manchester Piccadilly
(24 February)

I should have been here yesterday but Doris had other ideas.

Storm Doris brought the country to a standstill. My train - or, as it turned out, my several trains and buses - was nine and a half hours late into Manchester. Staying again with Lynne and David, I sent messages; so did everyone else in the country as the nation was stuck. David had made our packed lunches, including Rosie's delectable banana cake. He stayed at home waiting - and waiting - to go walking with me. Eventually he went to see the Halle Orchestra instead.

He couldn't come today so he gave me both the packed lunches. I ate them before eleven o'clock.

Skirting Stockport's Mersey Square, where I used to sell *Socialist Worker* on a Saturday morning, I followed the 192 bus all the way to Manchester. En route I called in at Levenshulme, where I worked forty years ago with the single homeless. It brought back good and bad memories, quite a lot of both.

The house on Grange Avenue is now a suburban semi-detached like any other. The two connected houses on Beech Range look as if they are still a hostel of some sort. I shudder to think of some of the things I did there: the night I threw a bucket of cold water over a woman who wouldn't sober up; of asking (no, instructing) two young people to have quieter orgasms; of the scar on my forearm; of being greeted with 'oh no, not you again' on Ward G2 (g for gynaecological) of the Manchester Royal Infirmary. At Grange Avenue, a very nice neighbour used to give me advice over the garden fence on gynaecological matters, a subject on which I was woefully ignorant (still am). But most of the time it was by guess and by God (just an expression...).

For a year I worked about ninety hours per week. After that time it came down to about sixty, plus of course actually living there as well. But then there was that one glorious respite between one house being closed down and the next unexpectedly taking eight months to open. They found me somewhere to live and told me to make myself scarce. So it was cricket three times a week for Chorlton and for Northenden bus depot (with my friend Derek, who was so shocked or disgusted at my appearance that he gave me two of his old inspector's jackets to wear as best), tennis almost every day, cinema, walking in the hills. It was the time of my life.

I wonder how many of the staff and residents of those hostels are still alive. One worker from another house was later murdered, another took his own life. Many of the residents must be dead. But we saved some lives too.

It was formative.

Day 120: Manchester Piccadilly to Rochdale
(10 March)

Not far from Piccadilly station lies Rochdale Road, a nice big main road that will assuredly take you to Rochdale, the place you want to go to. Fortunately Julia blew that one out before we started.

My cousin Julia joined me for most of the day and she knew the way. Above all, she knew there was a canal.

We had to join it in Ancoats and, to make sure we were going the right way, we asked directions from a couple of police officers. I mention that only because they were the first police I have met so far on this trip who have not immediately apprehended me.

The canal was unmemorable. Most of the detritus of the western world lined its banks. Male ducks fought and pursued lone females, who dived for refuge under the water. Spring is here.

Julia and I exchanged information: family news, family dynamics, politics, history, books, plays and all the rest. We had a coffee, a tea and our packed lunches. (I stayed with Lynne and David again last night.) Eventually Julia had to go. We worked out where we were on the map and she went off to catch a bus. Then I realised we were somewhere else entirely so I hoped she got home.

The canal climbed. It crossed fields, railway lines, rivers and huge roads. I had an unintended tour of Rochdale as I sought the station. I know just as much about Rochdale today as I did yesterday: nothing.

It's been a strange few days. I had some work in Blackburn on Thursday and work in Bridgend on Monday. Then back here.

Day 121: Rochdale to Todmorden
(11 March)

The canal banks are not picturesque; they are not picture postcard. That doesn't matter; they are not there to look pretty. One feature, however, does stand out above all others. Dog shit. Seldom is the dog shit totally ignored by the dog owner. It would be better if it was. Instead, it is dutifully wrapped in little black bags. Then it is left. Is it left in an appropriate litter bin? No. Is it taken home? No. The path is festooned with little black plastic bags full of mouldering dog shit. If all that shit was just left alone on the path it would decompose and fertilise. Wrapped in plastic bags it is just adding to the plastic mountain. A shitty one.

On the plus side, who should come storming over the horizon but my Companion? Cruising at twice my speed, Mother Goose-like in her concern for my welfare, back in her native county she was uncontrollable. We followed the canal from Rochdale to Littleborough, had lunch in an excellent café, then went over the top via the Littleborough Summit. Thirty locks took us up and then down again. These canals are anything but flat.

Henrietta and Frank knew everyone within ten miles who has ever been to a gig, read a book, written a poem or started a business. They were also generous hosts.

Todmorden is, as everyone acknowledges, populated by people who can't afford Hebden Bridge. However, it is also rather nice. All the villages round here are a bit dark and gloomy but they are also impressive to look at and increasingly cultural. Music and literature thrive.

Place name of the day: Bottoms.

Heard next day: 'My parents would literally bend over backwards.' Let's hope they didn't have to.

Days 122-123: Todmorden to QUEENSBURY
(31 March and 1 April)

Oh dear oh dear. Another setback. Well, two setbacks.

The first arose from medical incompetence. Mine. Sitting watching TV one night, my attention wandered (which normally means I'm asleep, but not this time) and instead of taking 6x2 mg of my Parkinson's pills I took 6x50 mg of my heart pills. Uh oh.

I rang the help line and was advised to take myself to A&E. I was in the area of Barnet Hospital, where the staff were of course superb. I stayed in overnight while they did the usual checks, then in the morning I toddled out again. Whacked. I was slow for a week or so and now I'm gradually building up again.

The second setback was not my fault. In fact I deserve nothing but sympathy. Why? Because I am now, according to the Bible, officially dead. I have had my time. Three score years and ten.

Be that as it may, I have got to hang on until I have finished the Qs. From Todmorden to the unpronounceable Mytholmroyd was a few gentle downhill miles beside the canal. Then another night of hospitality from Henrietta and Frank, in the company of the erudite Paulette. Then my Companion, newly arrived, and the most important dog Magic and I attacked the numerous contour lines between Mytholmroyd and Queensbury.

Luddenden was nice and already up the hill. We went up a lot more hills after that and passed through Mixenden, which frankly wasn't very nice. But the dog didn't mind. Climbing up rough ground towards Queensbury he pursued a couple of deer which were about forty times his size. All three of us were pooped by the time we reached Queensbury but only one of us stretched out prone on the pub carpet, tongue lolling. Which showed great restraint.

So we're at another Q. What is Queensbury like? Don't know. We saw nothing today except the inside of the pub. The area is hilly and heavily populated. Maybe next time.

There is a modern skill which I shall not attempt to master: using the urinal while simultaneously checking your mobile. Maybe it's a northern thing.

Day 124: Plan B: Northampton to Brixworth
(30 April)

What?

Desperate measures, desperate measures. I have decided on a twin pronged approach.

Lancashire is, unfortunately, a bloody long way off (except from Lancashire) and needs three days on one trip to make it worthwhile. We Norfolk people find it hard in spring to take three days away (carrot topping, muck spreading etc.). But the trail of the Qs leads from Lancashire up to Durham then down through Lincolnshire and Leicester. So I'll try to fill in with some one day trips at the other end of the Qs. Places like Northampton are just down the road.

But there is a secret. A couple of years ago Scott was visiting London from Switzerland and wanted to go for a walk. So we took him to the Chilterns (more or less) and walked to a couple of letter Qs (which was just what he wanted to do, of course). They were Quainton and Quarrendon. I can't remember much about either of them. We did have a very nice lunch though.

That was two down anyway. Technically they ought to be joined to all the others but I'm afraid they may not be.

Next on the list is Quinton near Northampton, not to be confused with Quinton in the West Midlands. I didn't even go there today but will come back. Instead we took the dog to Northampton.

A very annoying verbal tic is people telling you that they 'have to say' something when they haven't to say anything of the sort. I have to say, however, that Northampton was dreary. But the dog had a high old time and we found our way out to the old railway track which was very pleasant. Then Brixworth.

Day 125: Brixworth to Market Harborough
(5 May)

Well, I enjoyed the tunnel - 480 metres in the dark.

I probably said last year - and the year before - that England in May is the most beautiful country in the world. This year the warm winter pushed everything forward, until the severe late frosts killed all the fruits and vines. Nevertheless the foliage and crops are in full bloom and the country is a riot of yellow and green. The wind was keen today but still this was one of the two days in the year when the north has better weather than the south. Here in the Midlands we are in the middle.

The Brampton Valley Way, or an equivalent, continued on the old railway line all the way to Market Harborough. It was idyllic. A lot of people had thought so too: benches with their dedications to former walkers dotted the path.

Then came the tunnel.

I have walked through tunnels in the Alps that went on for miles and were incredibly noisy, fume filled and dangerous. None of that applied here. There was another factor to make it a bit hairy though. It was dark.

There was light at the end of the tunnel - but no light in between. Notices warned of being run down by cyclists or pedestrians. I whistled and sang loudly and just avoided one of the cyclists. For some reason 'The Trolley Song' came to my lips. My dramatic interpretation of Judy Garland rang out. I emerged. I didn't go down the next tunnel.

Day 126: Market Harborough to Great Glen
(12 May)

Outside Market Harborough stands Gartree Prison. I wonder if they still have the netting over the exercise yard.

It was the most spectacular prison escape. The helicopter landed in the middle of the exercise yard and whoops, hey presto, off went the prisoner. He was an East End gangster, as it happened the probation client of one of my colleagues in north-east London. He was later recaptured, I think, but by that time he was a legend. They put netting over the exercise yard.

Later I had a client in Gartree, a tough young man who had served a few years. I asked him what he wanted to do with himself when he came out. He said he wanted to go to the theatre. Partly this was because he had never been. Partly it was because Felicity Kendall was on in the West End. Unfortunately her run had ended by the time he came out but he was still up for it. I said we could go to the theatre as our parole appointments. So we did.

He started work on a demolition site the day after he came out. That night we went to the theatre in Stratford, east London. We continued to do so until his parole ended satisfactorily. I don't know if he ever went to the theatre again but it was possibly the most useful work I ever did. In today's Probation Service it would probably get me sacked.

In Market Harborough I bought a pair of reading glasses (£1.99) and a basic map (£5.95), having left both behind. Finding them both took an hour, though, and it was after midday when I left town.

Market Harborough is pierced by the Grand Union Canal, a wonderful construction on which I have walked in the past from London to Milton Keynes. It is quiet, easy, convenient and beautiful. So I set out on the main road, which looked a lot straighter.

I have it on good authority (Mick Gough) that the Foxton Locks, which I thereby missed, are spectacular.

A very brief encounter with the road proved that it was impossible to walk along it, so I cut through to the Langtons (lots of Langtons) then turned for Kibworth and Great Glen. A man with a dog advised that I could walk along the main road for that stretch, but at the bypass I should climb over a fence and follow the parallel road. He was right. Whether he was legal was less certain.

Day 127: Great Glen to Leicester to Birstall
(18 May)

'Where am I?'

'You're in Birstall.'

Oh good. Actually I knew I was in Birstall and it was more a question of detail as I burst through the hedge from the steam railway track. The woman and child may have had a surprise at my sudden appearance but guided me imperturbably out of Birstall again via the bus.

Do they eat a lot in Leicester? Between Great Glen and Leicester seven conventional eating places invited the walker. From the edge of the city to the centre the same walker would be invited to eight Indian restaurants and those of some of the rest of the world's nationalities. That was just one side of the city; there were even more on the other side. How can the population keep all these restaurants going? Do they eat out three times a day?

But I ate in Sainsbury's café where I had a sensational lentil and dhal soup. You could eat it with a knife and fork.

The downside of the Sainsbury's experience was that a young woman came up and offered to tie my straggling shoe lace for me.

'Do I look that frail?' I asked.

'Yes,' she said.

I thanked her, I hope genuinely, but said I could manage.

Leicester has leading football, cricket and rugby teams. It is also in the top division of Indian food. I walked through the middle of town, following the A6. Suburbs came and went. The Grand Central steam railway allegedly starts at Leicester North but was like the *Mary Celeste* today. That was Leicester.

It was a painful day because I was wearing the wrong boots and got a blister.

Place name of the day: Kirby Muxloe.

Day 128: Birstall to QUORN (QUORNDON) to Sileby
(20 May)

I once went to Antigua to see Viv Richards bat for the Leeward Islands against England. When I arrived I discovered he wasn't playing. 'Rested.' (But I did later meet his brother, courtesy of my friend Jomo who went to school with him.)

Another time I was on Saturday court duty in Walthamstow when Brian Lara was batting for Warwickshire against Middlesex at Lord's. I wrapped up the court duty very swiftly and rang Lord's to see if he was still batting. Yes, he was. I flew.

When I arrived he was on 135.

He was out for 137.

Today was up there with those achievements. The great Kumar Sangakkara, the world's most beautiful batsman, was batting for Surrey against Middlesex. Overnight he was on 113. I was in London so got on the bus. Arriving at the ground a few minutes late, I checked the score before getting off again.

Sangakkara was out for 114.

I stayed on the bus. They had a perfectly good day's cricket but I didn't want to see it. I went walking in Leicestershire instead.

Is it Quorn or Quorndon? Is it one place or two? Have I missed Quorndon if I just go to Quorn?

I think - and I stress the word think - that it is all the same place. In this case I have knocked two Qs off the list at one fell swoop. How many are left? I will have a count up. Until now I have never dared look, but doing two at once has made me, well, optimistic.

I wandered up to Quorn via the villages, sheltered in the pub for an hour while it piddled down, then retraced my steps (always hateful) through Mountsorrel to Sileby. At the edge of town a good quality cricket match was defying the wicket, which resembled a green plum pudding.

Q

Quadring (Lincs)
Quadring Eaudike (Lincs)
Quaking Houses (Durham)
Quarrington (Lincs)
Quarrington Hill (Durham)
Quebec (Durham)
Queenstown (Lancs)
Queniborough (Leics)
Quernmore (Lancs)
Quinton (Northants)

That's about it. Queniborough here I come.

Day 129: Sileby to QUENIBOROUGH to Rearsby
(13 June)

There has been another setback.

A couple of weeks ago, apropos of nothing at all, my heart went wrong again. It is about a year since the last time so it is back to the regime of pills and amino acid powders and there will be no proper exercise including walking. Certainly anything uphill is out of the question; I can't walk upstairs. So that's put the kibosh on Lancashire. What else is possible? Somewhere with no hills at all? Head for the fens!

Very, very, very slowly I trudged out of Sileby. Local information indicated that the path went all the way to Syston through the lark-nesting wheat fields. (Incidentally how do the larks ever find their nests again among all that identical wheat?) I slid into a mud puddle under a road bridge and couldn't get out again. Eventually I extricated myself via a patch of stinging nettles. It was all squelchy.

Queniborough, the promised land! It seemed fairly ordinary. I went on to Rearsby and even scouted beyond to see if the main road had a footpath beside it. Answer: no it hadn't. I shall have to double back to Thrussington and the villages.

Three very gentle hours felt like ten. I had set June aside to finish this venture but that is a very long way from reality. The body has caught up with me.

I saw someone spend £41 in Poundland. I wouldn't have thought this possible.

Day 130: Rearsby to Melton Mowbray
(19 June)

The Co-op in Asfordby was delightfully cool. Everywhere else was hotter than hell. It was over thirty degrees.

Last night I won £41 in the hundred club in the pub at home. That made life better.

The hottest place I have ever been was Khartoum; travellers were complaining that the showers in Khartoum weren't as cold as the showers in Cairo. Honduras was pretty warm too; I had to get up regularly during the night to take cold showers. Asfordby was next in line. (No it wasn't.)

Melton Mowbray was not far along the main road but a few miles further through the villages. Very, very slowly (only two verys today) I progressed past a holiday and water activities area. Thrussington and Hoby also seem to be centres of the skittles world. Not many people know that.

Asfordby was followed on the map by Asfordby Hill. Uh-oh. Yes, there was a hill, on which I had to stop three times. Roll on those fens. I ate tortilla chips, chocolate and ice cream and followed my nose into Melton.

Melton Mowbray is, so they say, the home of Stilton cheese and pork pies. It seems a pleasant market town. To support the local economy I bought a £2.30 piece of Stilton. It melted in my bag. The plan was to eat it with cauliflower in the evening. I didn't have the energy to cook the cauliflower so I gnawed at them both on the sofa.

Place name of the day: Frisby on the Wreake.

Day 131: Melton Mowbray to Colsterworth
(23 June)

I had never heard of Colsterworth and I just could not remember the name. The same has happened with other, larger places that I have walked towards: most notably Tegucigalpa (capital of Honduras) and Podgorica (capital of Montenegro, much easier when it was Titograd). I walked towards Tegucigalpa for five days and still couldn't remember it; even now it sometimes eludes me. Colsterworth will not be signposted for five days. Or even five minutes.

From Melton Mowbray it is thirteen miles. This used to be a fleabite. When I walked across the US I averaged twenty-five miles per day and sometimes did thirty-five. Even the walk to Turkey averaged about twenty. But I was thirty-seven years younger in the US and I was still healthy on the road to Istanbul. Thirteen miles today took me nearly six hours.

Some years ago I was in a car with three other men on the way to a tennis match in Corby when a bird with an enormous wingspan rose from the ground. 'That's a kite!' we all cried, though none of us, I think, had ever seen one before. Today one hovered near me, even came down to take a look. Perhaps I was moving so slowly that it thought I was road kill.

Where are those bloody fens? The countryside did a lot too much undulating. Until a track before Buckminster, the route lay entirely on the B676. These B-roads are generally inauspicious: as busy as A-roads but without the protection. It was hard, busy and dangerous and I spent the afternoon leaping into the verge.

Buckminster provided an apple, a banana, a cup of tea and a Magnum classic, all purchased in the village shop. Tea was Indian-style, meaning that if you ask for no sugar you get one sugar; it is inconceivable that anyone could want no sugar at all. The shop had become the village meeting place, where people gathered to discuss their operations and children. I overheard one conversation which I thought was about children. 'I've got one at the minute. Steve's got two. I sold one.' It was about BSA motorbikes.

The lady of the shop even offered me a lift to Colsterworth, which of course I declined.

The A1 runs beside Colsterworth and I had assumed there would be buses running up and down all the time. Wrong again. I asked in the Co-op. No-one knew bus times but it seemed possible there was one going into the back of beyond and the last one had gone to town. (Six o'clock.) I was standing outside looking bemused and wondering whether to go to Back of Beyond when one of the Co-op customers stopped his car and kindly offered a lift to a station. Well, yes please, thank you very much indeed. I would come back next time.

Day 132: Back to Plan A: Queensbury to Oxenhope
(30 June)

Heard the one about the bluff Yorkshireman?

I had some union business in Preston yesterday so I took the opportunity to go back to Plan A for a few hours: that is, taking the Lancashire bit instead of the Lincolnshire bit. The train dropped me in Halifax and I caught the bus to Queensbury, where we finished last time.

The bus had a bus driver and the bus driver was bluff.

Unfortunately my bus pass had a crack in it and it wouldn't work the machine. Well, to Mr Bluff this was not an unlucky accident or even a freak of nature, but a very personal insult to the bus company, to the Almighty and, far worse, to Yorkshire; so he levelled some very personal insults at me. If anyone had spoken to me like that in Norfolk I would have hidden under the seat. But he wasn't, of course, being a rude bastard who ought to learn some manners. He was just a bluff Yorkshireman.

Everyone else was very nice to me. Perhaps he was too. It was for my own good.

Apparently Queensbury is the highest town in the something or other: West Riding or Yorkshire or England. It is certainly high, approached on one side from a long elevated ridge. It doesn't have a lot more for the passer-by to talk about. It isn't wealthy.

This was my first day in the hills since my heart went wrong again; all I attempted was a few miles as gently as possible. The main road took me most of the way, then a bridleway led into the hills. This was moorland. At the far end of a reservoir the footpath signs led straight ahead. If I had taken them I would still be going there, but after a few minutes I realised they brought nothing but emptiness. I turned back and took the obvious way towards the valley.

A pack of Yorkshire terriers nipped at my ankles, either in affection or in loathing. I asked their owner how many he had got. 'I'm not sure,' he said. 'Hard to tell.' At least ten anyway. I didn't point out that I was on a public footpath and that they were biting me. He was giving me directions.

Oxenhope was supposed to be the final staging post on the way to Haworth, the destination for the day. At the bus stop, however, stood a man who stated authoritatively that the only bus of the day was about to pass on its way to Keighley. This seemed an opportunity not to be missed. (I later discovered that he meant the only one by a particular route.) Lazy today means more work next time but it's always the same: choose the lazy option. I took the bus to Keighley and the train to

Skipton, whence Hugh took me to Barnoldswick to spend the night with him and Val.

I have known Hugh for fifty-two years.

Days 133-134: Oxenhope to Haworth to Stanbury
(27-28 July)

It was County Week.

Twice a year, for five days in summer and three in winter, all the county tennis teams in the country compete against each other in a succession of leagues. The competition is intense, the standard incredibly high, the tension often unbearable as the week reaches a climax and your team can go up, stay the same or go down. I watched Norfolk women at Cromer for the first two days and then Norfolk men at Ilkley.

Ilkley, it turned out, was just round a couple of corners from Oxenhope.

There wasn't time to have a real walk and the body has yet to be tested properly, so I took the opportunity merely for a couple of miles each day. It was hilly. Haworth was, of course, full of tourists (like me). I didn't see any Brontes but went on the steam train back to Keighley, which, on a wet day with nowhere else to go, was chocker. Great enthusiasm was raised by my buying a single, one way ticket on the steam train. No-one appeared to have seen one of them before. Everyone goes for a day trip, there and back again.

Haworth is pleasant and has incredibly helpful tourist information staff. They damn nearly came out and walked to Stanbury with me. However, I pushed slowly up the road alone, testing to see if this thing is doable. Down a hill, up a hill and there we are. It will give a good starting point for next time.

Norfolk women and Norfolk men both got promoted.

Days 135-136: Stanbury to Wycoller to Brierfield
(29-30 August)

We started at Stanbury. Hugh and Val started at Wycoller. The plan was to meet halfway.

Oops.

We were still on the edge of Stanbury when I looked up and saw two people looming on the road ahead, looking purposeful. It was them. They had already walked from Wycoller. Now, having reached Stanbury, they had to walk the whole distance back again. They were very understanding. Or too tired to protest. Since Val does fifteen miles on the moors every Wednesday, though, it was more likely to be the former.

The other week we met a woman who did ultra walking. She had done a non-stop 100 kilometres in about twenty-four hours. Next year she hopes to do 100 miles for which you are allowed twenty-eight hours.

I am in awe of people like her. The most I have done in a day is fifty miles once when I was seventeen. It was a long way. Probably my hardest day, though, was in Colorado when I walked about thirty-seven miles along roads climbing to eleven thousand feet; it snowed and I had to reach somewhere to stay the night. When I got there I couldn't eat. The body just couldn't deal with it.

Since we were so far behind with the schedule, we went in the pub.

After coffee and chat it was slowly up the main road until we could join the Bronte Way by the reservoir. This is stunning moorland scenery, bleak and bare, very much appreciated by the dog. Very slowly indeed we went up the hills, making kind allowances for my heart. We came down to the green sheltered grove of Wycoller.

Wycoller was a weaving town (that is, a town where there was weaving) in the eighteenth century; it was made redundant by the Industrial Revolution. Somebody or other built a hall there. In the twentieth century the local council made it into an activities centre. In the twenty-first century the cuts in local government took most of the activities away again.

We spent the night with Hugh at Barnoldswick, then I started again at Wycoller on the flat route. The plan is still to cosset the heart into submission.

Winewall was prosperous. Colne was not prosperous but had aspirations. Are there two theatres? The cricket ground was locked but through the gates was a view of a wonderful little ground, scene of thousands of hard fought Lancashire club matches over the last hundred years or more. Further on I hoped to see Nelson cricket ground where Learie Constantine worked his magic for a number of years. He also lodged in the town and local people used to peer into his window at night, having never seen a black person. Whirlwind batsman, whirlwind bowler and whirlwind fielder to boot, he later became a barrister and Trinidad & Tobago's High Commissioner in London. He also - a black man - captained the Commonwealth team that played England in the Victory test matches of 1946.

In the largest shop it has ever been my dubious pleasure to enter, my Companion was lining up a baked potato in the heaving cafeteria. Then we walked through Nelson. It has to be said (there you are again -does it have to be said?) that Nelson is as grim as they say. It is a very poor town. It is also a predominantly Asian town but that isn't its major characteristic. Grinding poverty overwhelms.

The local probation office has shut down. Victim of more cuts, the Probation Service has abandoned localism, community feeling and convenience in favour of clients ringing up to report in and going to prison if they don't. Not very useful or successful but who cares about that?

Day 137: Plan B, back to the lowkands: Grantham to Honington
(16 September)

It was described later, rather unkindly I thought, as a chain of incompetence. I prefer to think of it as a natural disaster.

I was in London overnight. In the morning I had a choice between turning left for the Overground or right for the

Underground to take me to King's Cross. I chose Overground and turned left downhill. When I arrived at the station I remembered that on Saturday the train ran at a different time. I had missed it. I belted back up the hill and all the way to the tube station. The trains were delayed - only slightly, but slightly was enough. I missed the train at King's Cross. By one minute.

The subsequent economical route to Grantham was far too long and circuitous to describe here. I got there an hour or two late and, instead of being very early for my bus to Colsterworth, I was an hour late; and there wasn't another one for several hours.

The only option was to forge ahead and fill in later: already knackered and feeling like a prat. If I could just get to Ancaster and catch the train back to Grantham, it would still have been quite a productive day.

I didn't even achieve that.

Grantham boasts the birthplace of Margaret Thatcher. Apparently there is some sort of memorial. I thought about vandalising it but decided that discretion was the better part of valour. A suitable memorial to Thatcher is the impoverishment of the town centre, matched by the prosperity of the outer suburbs. That's what she did to the country.

A footpath lay beside the main road all the way so there was no difficulty of choice. A week or so ago, I went to a talk by John Pepper, the eighty-two-year-old advocate of fast walking to cure the symptoms of Parkinson's. Again I belted along, partly in anger at my own inadequacies, partly in fury at Thatcher, partly in an attempt to follow John Pepper. Through the stone villages of Belton (stately home) and Barkston. Up to Honington. Forty-five minutes until the train left Ancaster. Could I do it?

No. I would be left stranded, watching the train in the distance. I spent those forty-five minutes waiting for the bus instead. Life is too short to spend forty-five minutes waiting for a bus in Honington.

Nothing against Honington, of course.

Day 138: Colsterworth to Grantham
(26 September)

A walk down Dovedale is quite different from a walk up the A1. That's my opinion after doing both.

Amazingly, from Great Ponton into Grantham the main road has a footpath beside it, though I doubt whether a pedestrian has ever been spotted there. A mile or so of this is the A1. Walking up the A1 is quite an extraordinary experience. It's rather busy. In one direction it says London. That's easy enough to grasp. In the other direction it indicates The North. This is a nebulous concept; the thing is, you never get there. You drive and you drive and still it says The North. And the whole world is going there. Well, one half is going to London, the other half is going north.

I spent the early afternoon trying to write jokes for a Welsh comic who won't want them. But it passed the time and made me laugh. (Mad walker seen laughing again.)

A couple of brown army jeeps went past, all vehicles and occupants heavily camouflaged for warfare in the arid brown desert. Let's hope no-one attacks them in the green, verdant landscape of Lincolnshire.

Easton has a walled garden which I didn't see. Great Ponton has a manor house which was closed today. That was about it. Where are those nice flat fens?

Day 139: Plan A, back in Lancashire: Brierfield to Accrington
(1 October)

Hugh was singing in Deansgate.

The Conservative Party conference was taking place in Manchester and a massive demonstration was happening outside. I was in London for a memorial picnic the day before, then catching the train up through Manchester to Brierfield. Serendipity suggested that between stations I could join the demo and even see Hugh's choir singing in support.

They cancelled my train. There was talk of a broken rail but I expect it was a conspiracy.

The woman sitting next to me was reading the political columns of the *Times* and *Telegraph* and was in a great hurry to get there. Maybe she was an MP. I did not start advocating the nationalisation of the railways: an opportunity missed.

Eventually I went via Preston, bypassing Manchester altogether, and started the day's walking very late.

The picnic had been to commemorate the great Tim Mara, who died twenty years ago aged forty-eight. A few days earlier I went to a funeral at home of someone who lived in the village all her eighty-odd years. For both occasions the community turned out: two very different communities but equally a part of my life. On both occasions, also, I was struck with the feeling: carpe diem, seize the day. There isn't long, make the most of it.

I jettisoned all my route plans for the next two days. The weather today was miserable and tomorrow they forecast everything short of the wrath of God. There was no obvious route and I didn't fancy getting blown away on some wild and woolly hillside, not to mention getting lost. I would take the main road. Sorry Whalley, sorry Longridge.

Anyway, Burnley has been home to romantic football styles and stories since the 1950s. Surely it must be a very romantic place?

I couldn't count the number of takeaways on the road in to Burnley. Striking, too, was the number of barbers open on a Sunday afternoon. Romantic, though? It is, of course, in the eye of the beholder.

I missed the town centre. At least I think I missed the town centre.

A couple of surprises lay between Burnley and Accrington. First, the road climbed almost up to the moors. Second, I seemed to reach Hapton at least three times, making it a much longer evening than a chap would want. The road passed the very tempting Agra restaurant; I once walked from Agra to Delhi.

It was dark well before Accrington station, which incidentally was half way up a mountain. I went off to the dive I had booked in Blackburn for the night, to return tomorrow.

Day 140: Accrington to M6
(2 October)

A year ago on Blackburn station I met a young man wearing Norwich City colours and reading *The Odyssey*. I told him it must be unusual to be wearing NCFC colours and reading *The Odyssey* on Blackburn station. He said he wanted to follow Norwich City and read the classics. He worked in a warehouse or similar. I asked if he had ambitions in life; he said he didn't really except for the above. I asked if his parents had been ambitious for him. He said they hadn't; but he added that he sometimes thought perhaps they should have been.

Norwich City had won convincingly that day. No doubt Odysseus had done the same.

On the way in to Blackburn, the Lettuce Leaf café was setting up for the day. The two owners worked on the principle that if the customer wanted something, they would try to supply it. You could ask for any dish in the world.

They said Blackburn was a nice town, quite small, with only one Matalan - the gauge these days. Their parents came from Kashmir and we had a chat about politics, heritage and all the rest.

A man in a pub pointed out the direction of Preston Old Road. I finished up on Preston New Road, a different matter, and walked as far as the footpath allowed. From the junction with the A59, just before the M6, the route will have to divert on the back roads into Preston.

Day 141: Plan B, Lincolnshire: Honington to Rauceby
(9 October)

Tantalisingly, Quarrington was in sight by the end of day 142.

But it was not a good day.

On a heroically circuitous route from Ullswater, my Companion dropped me in Honington, Lincs. It was almost five in the afternoon when I set off from there, a ridiculous time of day at this stage of the year. I wanted to close a chapter by reaching Sleaford via Quarrington and I thought I saw the opportunity to do so. However, like most half-baked schemes it remained half-baked.

All the way from Grantham and beyond, a cycle and footpath had run beside the road; I was confident that it would continue to Sleaford.

You should always be confident.

It lasted for about a hundred yards. I spent the rest of the day hopping into the verge. In the dark.

I had calculated that it would be dark at seven o'clock. I was right. But it was also dark quite a long time before seven o'clock. It was pitch dark at seven o'clock but highly unsuitable for walking some time before that. Eventually I decided it was too dangerous to make Sleaford that night.

The arrival of a train at Rauceby station is not so unusual; it happens at least twice a day. What is unusual is that there is a person working at Rauceby station. This is not in order to sell tickets, make the customers feel at home or anything as arcane as that. It is to climb down out of the signal box and open the manual gates whenever a train passes through. The man also unlocked the gates to the platforms, otherwise no-one would ever have caught one of those two trains. He shouted useful information from the heights of his signal box. It was like going back to a Will Hay film.

Endless research (by someone else) had indicated that a train might be coming around that time. It came indeed. I still dallied with the idea of trying to make Sleaford tonight on foot despite the dark, but if I didn't make it for the train connection there I would have to spend the night in Sleaford: a fate far, far worse than death. I climbed on to the train at Rauceby.

Day 142: Rauceby to QUARRINGTON to Sleaford
(13 October)

Now where exactly was Quarrington?

I was in the area so took the opportunity to polish off the end of the previous day. It should be no more than an hour's walk. Let's see when the trains go. Well, one went in a few minutes time to Sleaford, just before six o'clock; and one came back in the morning.

Oh dear oh dear, it's back to walking in the wrong direction again. I thought I had given that up. I took the train to Sleaford and walked back.

It was dark.

There was a sign saying Quarrington but it was on the railway line rather than the road. On the road at the turning for Greylees (where Rauceby station actually is) there is a road sign saying Quarrington half a mile. If this was the case, I had just walked through it. But there was nothing there. On the map it is quite a big place. In reality it doesn't exist. Well, if it does I can't find it.

This bit is really rather boring, but sometimes life is like that.

Day 143: Plan C: QUINTON to Northampton
(15 November)

No, I hadn't forgotten Quinton...

First, I heard in quick succession two of the worst couplets in pop music.

Yeah, my heart stood still
Yeah, his name was Bill.
The Crystals, 'Da Doo Ron Ron'

As if that wasn't bad enough:

I will give you my finest hour
The one I spent watching you shower.
Blondie, 'Picture This'

I looked up the distance from Northampton to Quinton. It gave me North Korea rather than Northampton. I tried again and it said seventy-one miles. What? Ah, it was the other Quinton, the one in the West Midlands. When I got the right one it said about five miles. Even after I got lost in Northampton it was only six or seven.

Nobody had ever heard of Quinton. Even the bus company that went there wasn't too sure. Apparently a new company has taken over and the drivers don't know the way yet. However, a ticket seller at the railway station went beyond the call of duty, found a map on the computer and told me which bus to catch and where.

I can't remember whether I am supposed to be walking from Northampton to Quinton or vice versa. It's all so long ago. But I know this is the penultimate tendril to be mopped up. After this there is just Plan A and Plan B.

Why have I fallen so far behind again over the last few weeks? I have been to Switzerland and I have done a bit of work (not in Switzerland) and I have been to England's finest second hand bookshop, Scrivener's in Buxton, and I have been in a unit called AEC (Ambulatory Emergency Care) at King's Lynn hospital where they were brilliant and I am now on a lot more medication and I had a heart monitor later for twenty-four hours and I am having all my dental fillings replaced in case it was the mercury that gave me the PD. So I have got a set of excuses but in reality it has probably been the same old self-indulgence, and moral turpitude, of course.

I got off the bus at the edge of Quinton and walked back through the nondescript area to Northampton. A bunch of very, very small children were selling buns for Children In Need. The buns are probably called cupcakes in the latest Americanism. They were very nice.

I think there are seven letter Qs remaining: two in Lancs, three in Durham (Plan A) and two in Lincs (Plan B).

At my annual trade union conference I was talking to Kath, who said she was looking for a project. Then she said that walking round the letter Qs sounded good and she would talk to her mate about it.

Yes! It's going to catch on!

But I had better get a move on or they will overtake me.

Day 144: Plan B: Sleaford to Heckington
(29 November)

Last night in the pub we were looking over an old Westacre cricket scorebook. Despite his protestations that he would not remember anything of his feats thirty years ago, Gordy could describe every ball. Then he asked what I was doing at the moment and I told him my plans for today. 'You're not still doing that, are you?' he said.

Earlier I had been to the Swaffham cobbler, the genius who patches up my walking boots year after year. (Is there anyone else who mends walking boots?) He asked where I was walking these days. When I told him I was still on the Qs, his expression was one of sympathy above all. At least I think that's what it was.

I missed all the planned transport connections and finished by walking from Heckington to Sleaford rather than vice versa. I was pretty cheesed off that it was only going to be a few miles. As it turned out, it was extremely fortunate.

Walking in the fens is a nightmare. (Some would say that anything in the fens is a nightmare. Not me, of course.) There are very few ways across and they are generally huge great main roads. You go down a promising minor road, it lasts for several miles and then you find yourself in some bloody great dyke. (Incidentally, that seems to be where most of the locals finish up too. The local news tonight gave two deaths, one in a river and one in a dyke, which appears to be the daily average.) I could find no way on the map of doing the next step so I set out from Heckington more in hope than expectation, fuelled by an onion bhaji sandwich from the Co-op. The wind was spiteful and snow is forecast for tonight.

Outside Heckington, a footpath was indicated next to the railway line. Despite all previous experience, I was buoyed into thinking that at last a footpath and I might be going in the same direction. Indeed we did for about fifty yards. Then it disappeared into a ploughed field.

I crept round the edge of the field but still had to walk through ploughed land for half a mile or so. It felt like a lifetime spent in a vat of porridge. Huge clods of wet earth clung to my heels, toes, sides, tops and bottoms. This was not the time of year to be walking through sodden heavy fenland soil.

Eventually and very slowly I escaped back to the roads. I crawled into Sleaford almost literally, bending forward and looking like everything I didn't want to look like. I may be biased but Sleaford is not at the best of times a place to make your heart soar. Not a day to be repeated.

Day 145: Plan A: M6 to Preston
(6 December)

It was a strange way to spend a December evening. A bit of work had taken me to Manchester and it seemed a good idea to fit in some walking, particularly if I could cover the bits that no-one else would ever want to accompany me on.

It was dark when I started and it was dark when I finished. Wandering out of town to see what happened, it transpired that a footpath led beside the main road all the way to the M6, through takeaway suburbia and then some woods. Just before the motorway stood a bus stop to take me back; the time table said a bus was due. I wasn't absolutely sure I was looking at the M6 so nipped across the road to read the big sign on the other side. Yes, you guessed it. While I was nipping, the bus came past. I had to walk all the way back to Preston.

At least that made up for not crossing the motorway to the exact spot where I finished last time. Made up for it many times over in fact, so there.

Day 146: Preston to Kirkham
(8 December)

The Station Hotel, Preston, is perhaps the cheapest hotel in the country. It is not the most luxurious but you get what you pay for. I have been here a number of times before but have never previously stopped for more than one night; two nights stretches the patience of both sides.

In the freezing breakfast room I came across a dapper but elderly Scotsman nursing a cup of tea. He had been stranded in Preston the night before because snow had interrupted the service to Glasgow. Someone had pointed out the place where he could get a couple of pints and he had ended up staying the night. All well so far.

At 2 o'clock in the morning he fancied a smoke. Seeing the notices in his room ('did ye know they call the police if ye smoke?'), he had gone downstairs to the back door and stepped outside.

And the door closed behind him...

The rest of the night he spent on the station. Frozen stiff. At five they opened the waiting room. At seven he got back into the hotel with the cleaners. He was waiting to see the landlady to discuss several matters.

I made my way out to the main road, past the place where I visited the local union branch a few months ago. (Oh all right, I made a speech.) My intention today was to walk if possible to Lytham, amble along the coast and catch the train back. However, at the major junction a few miles outside Preston two things were clear: first, Lytham was too far, and second, that road didn't have a cycle path beside it whereas the Kirkham road did.

It was hard to believe that the village of Clifton could sustain Matt's Café (or anyone else's) but he was doing a busy trade. He was exchanging musical beliefs with a customer when I entered. Which was the best decade, 1980s or 1990s? Timorously I enquired about the 1960s, did he know about them? Matt (assuming it was he) looked at me with consternation. All right, point taken.

The scenery between Preston and Blackpool vies with the fens. I'll say no more than that. Pylons improve it. Kirkham Prison is one that I was lucky enough never to visit and I didn't see it today. On the way in to Kirkham a very knowledgeable passenger at a bus stop gave me a list of all the buses that hadn't been running, probably due to adverse weather; so I joined him on the one that came along just then. Snow lies to the north, snow lies to the south and pretty soon, they say, it will lie here too.

It might seem cheap to describe as a bastard the guard on Northern Trains who, despite the chaos and delays, charged me a fresh ticket to travel on his train instead of another one which hadn't materialised. As soon as I reached Manchester Oxford Road, the staff there and on a different company were as sweet as a nut.

Place name of the day: Newton with Scales.

Day 147: Plan A: Kirkham to QUEENSTOWN to Blackpool
(29 December)

An extraordinary day.

Bands of snow lay across the country from left to right. West to east. None lay in central Lancashire, but instead stinging rain flew from a gale force wind. It wasn't a cheerful scenario.

Then it did cheer up. Past a junction and round a corner, what was that in the distance? Was it a pylon? No, it was too solid. How high was it? It was tall and it was shapely. Where were we? Not in Paris certainly, but there was a similarity when seen from a very long way off. It must be Blackpool Tower!

It was a long time coming.

On the road, cones and barriers indicated road works. So did notices warning of pedestrians in the road. In a field on the other side of the road, some sort of industrial plant or machinery was working away. Then on the near side a small shelter of some sort housed a few women and one man. There were no road works in sight. What was going on?

It was fracking.

Across the road, in the field they were fracking. On this side of the road was the anti-fracking movement. A full anti-fracking camp was set up on a local farm. By the road was the front line.

They gave me a cup of tea and we talked. They monitored everything the fracking company did, every movement and use of machinery, and posted it on the internet daily. Each time they posted anything significant, the company's shares went down. Investors thought it was a loser.

They also stopped the traffic (almost all of which was sympathetic) and they blocked the fracking company's lorries. While I was there, the man in the group took a billboard and walked up the middle of the road with it. It seemed to get a good reception. Everyone in Lancashire appears to be against fracking. So why is it happening?

Meanwhile one of the women looked at me intently. 'I know you,' she said. 'We have met before. I know we have.'

It took a while to sort out when and where. I was convinced she had got the wrong man. Then someone else mentioned her name. Ah-ha! I represented Simone for our trade union not long ago in another part of the country. We only met once, then did everything by correspondence, which was my excuse for not recognising her. It was the wildest of coincidences that brought us together now in central Lancashire. We talked. She praised my emails.

At this stage of her life, Simone had exchanged working in the courts for appearing in court. A whole bunch of them were charged with various offences like obstruction and, under anti-trade union legislation, 'depriving a workman of his tools'. They were all pleading not guilty.

Reluctantly I moved on and made my way to Blackpool where I got lost. You might think this impossible, given that the sea was on one side and land on the other. Yet I seemed to go in endless circles. I was looking for Queenstown. The first four people I asked, all of them local, had never heard of it. The fifth was authoritative but gave me street names that never materialised. I thought I had missed it altogether. Later, looking at the map, it appeared that I had either been through the fringes or been within a hundred yards of them. It was just a part of Blackpool really. That would have to do.

Blackpool is itself extraordinary. This is midwinter in a northern seaside resort. It should be closed and indeed half of it is. The other half is throbbing. Much of this consists of cheap guesthouses and chippies. There are also monstrous hotels. I am staying in the most monstrous of them all (cheap deal). Many of the hotels insist on a minimum booking of seven nights at New Year. Seven nights? People come here for seven nights in the middle of winter in the wind and the rain, with Storm Dylan and Storm Eleanor brewing?

Several times I circled the tower without ever actually reaching it. Finally I set off north up the seashore, getting blown into the street for the first time since thirty-three years ago by the Bora wind in Croatia. I stopped to ask how far it was to my monstrous hotel. Ten-minute walk apparently. Twenty minutes later I asked again. Ten-minute walk, yes I guessed it. Fifteen minute later I arrived, very tired.

The place is full of children. A very small girl picked up some things for me from the floor. 'Thank you,' I said. 'You are very helpful.' 'I am helping you,' she replied, 'because I am bored.'

Day 148: Blackpool to Fleetwood (only)
(30 December)

Another oh dear.

I dawdled up the coast, breakfasting in Cleveleys and continuing up the spit of Fleetwood. I didn't seriously think I would reach Cockerham but I would get as far as possible and then catch the bus, coming back in the morning. First came the ferry from Fleetwood to Knott End, then the path along the coast.

Quite a lot of things were wrong with this plan. The first was that I arrived at the ferry station at 1.30 but they stopped running the ferry at 12.45.

Why? The time of year? The tide? Their mood? Or was it personal to spite me?

I have never had much luck with boats, possibly because I am scared of them. I would probably have been seasick on the Fleetwood ferry. My worst ever experience was in Guyana, where I tried to go up country to see Megan, daughter of my friends Nigel and Bridget. The canoe-type boat had a maximum capacity of eight but that day held twelve plus a large gas cylinder. We went out to sea where the engine failed. We were given tarpaulins as the waves crashed over us. We all thought we were going to die. The boatman turned for home and miraculously the engine worked again. I came home without ever seeing Megan. My only trip to rival it was from Union Island in the Grenadines to Carriacou. The safe part in the middle of the boat was full of Coca-Cola while the passengers clung to the outside, never letting go.

I do regret, however, turning down one boat trip. Walking down the street in Addis Ababa, I was approached by a youngish white man who asked if I knew anything about anthropology. I denied it. Did I know anything about archaeology? I denied that too. How about boats? Certainly not. Well, despite that would I like to go on a trip up the Omo? Thank you, but no I wouldn't. Half an hour later I changed my mind and went looking for the man; perhaps fortunately, I never found him.

Some would say Fleetwood was the end of the world. It is certainly the end of that part of the world. Its crowning glory is Rossall School, which looks like a cross between a prison and a workhouse. The eminent Fleetwood football team was playing today but not at home. I had a terrible portion of chips. What should I do next?

The distance I had walked from Blackpool would, if I had struck out inland, have taken me a long way towards Cockerham. There was, however, no way out of Fleetwood except backwards. I took the bus back to Blackpool and another bus to Lancaster to approach the problem from the other end.

Three buses meant three bus drivers. The first was dour but helpful. The second was a rude bastard. The third was, as I told her, an absolute star. I had reached Lancaster two hours early for her bus - all time that I could have spent walking - and I asked her what the prospects were for walking her route instead of waiting. She said that walking down that road in the dark I would undoubtedly be killed. When I later travelled along it in her bus I agreed with her.

She put me off at the luxury resort at Thurnham where I had got another deal to stay the night. I had an apartment with cooker, microwave, sunken bath and 100 channels of TV. I used the bath.

The bit I missed today is the only bit missing in the entire trip. That means I shall have to come back some time and do the bloody thing. But not tomorrow.

Day 149: Thurnham to Lancaster
(31 December)

I paid a tenner for a cup of tea and a cheese sandwich in a pub. Even that wasn't the worst part of the day.

I'm not going to write much about this.

I was almost too tired to reach Lancaster at all. It really wasn't very far and I had allowed lots of time until my train. Outside Galgate I met the canal, the first I have been on for ages and a real bonus. I wandered along, more and more slowly. By the time I reached Lancaster I was barely moving. Someone told me it was a mile and a half to the station. That would be an hour and a half then. I went in to the hospital to look for a taxi. No luck.

It was a fixed time train and I was going to be fifteen minutes late. I gave up and entered the pub. Later the booking clerk told me that that train was forty-five minutes late and I would have caught it easily.

The last time I was in Lancaster was to visit the prison. That was better than this.

Day 150: Lancaster to QUERNMORE
(8 February)

The weather forecasters said there would be a light rain for some of the time. They were absolutely right. What they didn't mention was that there would be a heavy rain for the rest of the time.

Frankly it pissed down.

On 11 March it will be five years since this venture started itself. I would really like to get shot of it by 11 March this year, which makes it inexcusable to have worked, read books, been to the cinema, gone on holiday or done anything else that I have dabbled with since my last visit.

My Companion and I arrived in Lancaster in mid-afternoon. An interesting contrast in styles meant that I followed the map and headed in completely the wrong direction, whereas she utilised all the modern technology and also took us in the wrong direction. After a bit of effing and blinding (on her part) we re-traced our steps and set off past Williamson Park and down the hill.

I have taken many wrong turnings in my time. Potentially the most serious was probably in Honduras. In a land without signposts I took the wrong fork one day in a forest. After an hour or two I came across a house and asked if I was going the right way. No, I was actually heading for El Salvador, about another hour away, where a war was going on and life was worth about the same as a Mars bar. I expressed my gratitude for the information and turned round.

Now we had to find Quernmore. Fortunately my friend Ewan, who comes from these parts, had told us how to pronounce it (Quorma, don't ask why), otherwise we might have been totally humiliated. In fact it was rather easy. It was particularly easy because my Companion took charge and carried all the gear.

Visibility was almost nil, similar to a Chinese smog, but still Quernmore was clearly a lovely spot: down a steep valley, round a stream and pond and up the other side. I posed at the village sign. That was far enough. I was struggling. Either the Parkinson's or lack of exercise or the wrong pill regime or all of the above seems to have done for me.

The plan was to walk on to Halton, cutting off some of the distance for the morning, but it was out of the question. Just the steep hill out of the valley nearly settled my hash for good and all. The only option was to walk back to Lancaster the way we had come. This would have been tedious on a warm sunny evening. There aren't really words to describe what it was like tonight.

Ewan joined us in the bar. His father used to be a probation officer in Lancaster and, in the old fashioned days when we were allowed to do useful work, he would take his clients out for the day to the Lakes. If he had space he might also take Ewan. One day Ewan was making a telephone call from a public call box, as you did, when suddenly the glass shattered and a gang of youths opened the door....

'Oops! Er, hello, it's Ewan... evening mate, you all right Ewan?'

During the evening my Companion heard that she has to go to a funeral in Belfast in three days' time and that her daughter Michelle had a car crash a couple of hours ago. And the food from our evening meal gave her an allergic gluten reaction. Apart from that it was a nice night.

Day 151: Lancaster to Carnforth
(9 February)

We didn't know which way to go. County Durham, where there are three letter Qs, is the target and I had planned a route leading diagonally across the Pennines via Kirkby Stephen. But I'm not sure I can do that at the moment. Ewan pointed out that the canal, which I had joined before, goes all the way to Kendal. Is that useful?

I didn't even look at the larger map. I didn't care if it lay in the right direction. If it was flat and promised a café from time to time, we were going there.

We went very, very slowly. Stunning views (I must stop saying stunning views) lay across Morecambe Bay to the snow covered mountains of the Lake District. Apparently the highest mountain visible from here is the Old Man of Coniston. My uncle Jim used to walk up it and run down it every morning before breakfast. Every morning. Until he was seventy.

Then we saw a goldcrest, my first ever. Chirpily eating berries from the hedge a couple of feet from the footpath, it wasn't bothered about us. Yes, we could see all its markings clearly. It was a goldcrest.

I hope it wasn't deceived by today's sunshine into thinking spring is here. The sky may be blue but the temperature is perishing and snow is due. The time has come to go south.

Our route to Carnforth was only eight miles but I was struggling. I realised tonight that I have actually hurt my back. Taking so many other pills I have given up the glucosamine, with dire consequences. I don't need consequences and will re-start tonight.

Carnforth is, of course, the setting of *Brief Encounter*. It has a heritage centre, a café and some old railway signs. Since balls were falling off brass monkeys, however, we didn't tarry. Dilys Powell, film critic of *The Sunday Times* when it was a newspaper, was right about most things and she hated *Brief Encounter*: thought it was turgid and boring. I met her once and she said so.

Day 152: Carnforth to Burton-in-Kendal
(15 March)

It was possibly the worst birthday of my life.

After a month of sitting about moping about the state of my body and mind, it was time to start again on this benighted venture. Had the body mended? Had the mind renewed? The answer to both questions came only too soon.

It's bad enough having a birthday at all when you're getting old. Nobody wants to be reminded, thank you. No-one wants to hear that terrible sympathy: 'Well, I hope I'm as fit as you when I'm your age', to which the obvious answer is: 'Just come and bloody try it then if it's so great.' Nobody wants to grow old at all, let alone have the ground cut away under their feet by failing to do even a short distance before curling up, bent over and staggering.

It was only a few miles along a nice, gentle canal. The first mile or two was fine. The third and fourth miles weren't too bad really. After that it was ... well, seeing as this was *Brief Encounter* land, it was a stiff upper lip situation.

The best thing to do is gloss over the next few miles. My Companion plus dog turned up and guided me, doubled up, into the service station which is supposed to be accessible only from the motorway. I subsided into a cup of tea while they brought the car illegally in the back way. Then we went off.

167

To make matters worse, some bright spark claimed recently on the radio that Norfolk has a second 'Q' place which I have never heard of let alone walked to. Allegedly it is called Quarles. Well, they can stuff that. They say it's a hamlet. It might as well be an omelette. I'm not counting it. It's not in my A-Z book of road maps. Up yours, Keith Skipper on Radio Norfolk.

Are things as bad as they seem?

Probably yes. Things are not good. On the other hand, recently I sent a piece to a travel magazine (which was not in the least interested). It perhaps puts the present situation into perspective. It was called 'Your Position Is Hopeless'. Here it is.

It all began so well.

I changed planes in St Lucia, had a few hours to spare and went down to the beach, where I got into conversation with a music journalist. I wandered back to the airport which in those days was barely a couple of rooms. I went in and looked around.

An announcement came over the loudspeaker. 'Will passenger Cameron please come through to the departure lounge?'

I went through. As I entered, a pilot came in from the opposite door.

'Are you Mr Cameron?' he asked.

I admitted it.

'Let's go, shall we?' he said. He and I went out to the aircraft.

No-one else was aboard and we flew up the beautiful coast of St Lucia to Martinique. I sat at his shoulder in the eight-seater plane.

'Is it often empty?' I asked.

'Sometimes it's full, sometimes it's empty,' he said philosophically. It made no difference to him; he was just flying.

After a pleasant couple of days in Martinique I needed to reach Antigua for my flight back to Britain. I took a shared taxi from the market place to Martinique airport. With the other passengers I entered the airport buildings.

Then I realised I had left my jacket over the back seat of the taxi.

I went running after it but the driver had gone.

I sat down and weighed up the situation. Still with me I had my ticket from Antigua to Britain. What I did not have was my ticket from Martinique to Antigua. Furthermore I did not have my passport to get me there either.

Unable to get on the plane, I went back to the market place, trying to find my driver, trying to remember what his car looked like. He was nowhere to be found.

I went to the Town Hall to discuss the situation. Discuss it, what's more, in French.

The very helpful woman agreed with me. I could get home from Antigua but unfortunately I could not get to Antigua.

She added that because Martinique is technically a part of France I could probably get from there to Britain with the identification I still had with me. She asked what I had got. Yes, my Norwich library card might do the trick. But I didn't have a ticket home from there nor enough money to buy one.

Finally, Britain had no representation in Martinique. Zero. Nothing at all.

This was not looking good. I asked what I should do.

'Your position is hopeless,' she said.

I think I laughed. I think she did too. We looked at each other for a while and then I said I would go for a walk and consider my situation.

I went back to the market place and had a cursory look round. There, what did I see but a shared taxi with the hatchback open and my jacket draped over the back seat.

I made a dash for it,

'Hey, what do you think you're doing?' said the taxi driver – or something like that.

'It's mine, it's mine!' I cried.

'What'll you give me for it?'

'Anything, anything, what do you want?'

He just laughed. 'No, take it.'

So I did. I had missed that plane but I caught one the next day. Then I came home with my passport, my tickets and my Norwich library card.

Q

Day 153: Burton-in-Kendal to Holme
(17 March)

The Beast in the East has struck twice in a week. We were snowed in. The wind was like a circular saw. It was the coldest day I have ever known in Britain. When the heating gave out in the house it was definitely time to leave. With the aid of a dustpan (always well equipped) we managed to escape the building.

It was a case of getting back in the saddle. The distance scheduled to walk was minuscule but at least it was walked. It ran along the canal. It was warmer (relatively). The countryside was pleasant.

Over to the east, the countryside was anything but pleasant. The huge, statuesque slabs of Pennine hills looked ultimately forbidding. All over the fells, walkers dotted the snow. Are they crazy, these people? The wind alone would freeze the fires of hell.

The canal was easy enough. Apparently it was called the black and white canal because the boats took coal southwards and returned with lime. Near the end were the coke ovens; at least I think so. Some sort of ovens anyway.

Fortunately I didn't have to pronounce Holme; almost certainly I would have given away my foreign-ness and had to squirm and grovel in embarrassment. Holme in Norfolk is usually shrouded in sea mist and used to have a cricket pitch like a pudding. That was bad enough but far worse was your situation if you mispronounced the word Holme. It is not, repeat not, pronounced 'Home'. If you make this cardinal error, you give yourself away as pretentious, arrogant, stupid and - a summation of all three - a foreigner, that is a person from beyond the county boundaries. The 'l' is pronounced, as it is in the more famous Holkham a few miles along the coast. Everyone knows that.

We went south. It wasn't very warm there either.

Day 154: Plan B: Heckington to Donington
(possibly 22 March. Forgot to record it)

For various reasons, none of them creditable, I wasn't thinking of going back north for a few days. Instead I wanted to polish off the fens according to Plan B. I didn't manage that either.

Heckington is a hotbed of heritage. The station hosts a railway museum that showed few signs of opening. Across the street, though, was the only working eight-sailed windmill in the world. No, I didn't know this beforehand, but I picked up a brochure along with two very large scones.

The place was throbbing with life. Volunteers enthusiastically guided trippers round the establishment. They seemed keen in fact to help anyone anywhere and I realised that this was the place to give me guidance. The question was: could I cross the drain?

Or perhaps that should be: THE DRAIN.

Now, this is not a drain like the drain leading out of your bathroom. This is a drain that's forty feet wide. When they drained this land to claim it from the sea, they built these huge waterways. There aren't many ways across.

We settled down, the staff and I, to examine the situation. Maps were pulled out, heads were shaken. All the minor roads had one thing in common: they stopped dead at a thin blue line. THE DRAIN took no prisoners.

Two main roads were the only way across towards Donington, my minimum target for the day: the A52 or the A17. Both presented a miserable prospect. The A52 was my route and I spent the afternoon following the fields as near as possible to the road. A kind woman stopped to offer a lift, suggesting that I didn't look too great, but I tried to reassure her. Later I received a solicitous message from the windmill (not the windmill itself, silly - from the staff) asking how far I had got.

The trouble with minimum targets is that if you set a minimum that's as far as you get. Donington is a big village or small town. Either way, its last bus of the day would take me out of there. It would, that is, if I could find out where to get on it. The location of the bus stop was strictly on a need to know basis. If you took the bus every day, you knew where it stopped so you didn't need a bus stop sign. If you didn't take the bus then you didn't need to know. I asked half a dozen people, all of whom were sure they had seen a bus somewhere round there but none of whom were exactly sure where it had gone. Eventually I caught the bus because it stopped just beside where I was standing.

Day 155: Plan B again, in fact the end of Plan B: Donington to QUADRING to QUADRING EAUDIKE
(3 April)

If I was a perfectionist I would walk from here to Durham (or Durham to here) to join up the dots. This is a tendril of the Qs while the main trunk roars (slithers) into the three remaining places which are all in County Durham. I was in the area so it seemed a good idea to clean them up. No, I am not going to walk from Durham to here (or here to Durham). Really I wanted to finish the venture here. What better place to end a pilgrimage than Quadring (pronounced Quaydring) Eaudike? What could be more romantic?

Hmmm.

Apart from looking at the tulips, which aren't out yet, the only known reason for visiting this area is to stop at the colossal cafés on the A17 near the Holbeach junction. Everyone in the east of England has stopped there at some time or other. In summer they are like a factory.

Then there is the place which would be the place name of the day on any day when it was not competing with Quadring Eaudike: Bicker. It ought to be twinned with Loggerheads which I went through near Stoke. I didn't detour to see it.

Someone told me previously that Quadring was nice. Well, nice is perhaps taking it too far. It's not nasty. A mile and a half to the left is Quadring Eaudike which could claim to be nothing but a real plod.

Did I really need to explore the whole village? I decided to walk as far as the road sign saying I had reached Quadring Eaudike. I looked for it - turned a corner and looked again - but I was blowed if I could find it. This must be more of the need to know basis. If you live in Quadring Eaudike you know where you live so you don't need to be told you have arrived. If you don't live there, you have no reason to be told; no-one is ever going to visit Quadring Eaudike so mind your own business and bugger off somewhere else.

So I did. I plodded off back to the main road. If I somehow missed the village sign (or indeed the village), I'm sorry.

There are just the three left in Durham now. Forty-two down.

Day 156: Holme to Levens
(13 April)

Desperate measures. Trying to keep up with some sort of schedule, I am skipping a Norwich City home match tomorrow. I wouldn't say I want them to lose because I should hate to miss a win; but I shall be less upset if they do lose.

Waiting for the bus in Carnforth, the only place to be was the magnificent bookshop. They have a sense of priorities up there. A first edition of a Len Hutton was worth twice as much as a first edition of a Boris Pasternak.

It was quite nostalgic setting off from Holme, where we and the dog stopped in the pub last time. Milnthorpe, I was told was 'three miles away if you're walking.' And if you're not?

Better than this was the place name of the day: Whassett. It must be awkward if you get drunk and are trying to explain where you come from. 'Where did you say you live?' 'Whassett, officer.' 'I said where do you live. Don't keep saying whassit to me or I'll bloody arrest you.'

Six months ago I had all my mercury dental fillings removed, since mercury is said to be a cause of Parkinson's. Since then I have felt much, much worse, perhaps because mercury takes a long time to clear the system. Today things started to feel better. I was walking almost like a human being.

The towns and villages were pleasant enough though grey. Milnthorpe, Heversham, Levens. There seems to be a plethora of manor houses round here, the biggest of them, Levens Hall, open to the public. A rather beautiful river ran through the grounds. Levens is west of my route but was where I had found accommodation. Or at least I thought it was at Levens.

I must have asked half the population of Levens where the pub was. Without exception they gave me excellent directions. They even offered lifts, which I foolishly turned down. Without exception I got lost. Part of the trouble was that my information just gave the name Levens. It hadn't occurred to me that it would be nearly two miles away in the opposite direction. I had to walk two extra miles tonight, therefore, and I will have to walk two extra miles back in the morning. Four extra miles which I will claim back with a clear conscience when the occasion arises.

It is a tribute to the appetite of the human race that they will drive to an obscure dump in the back of beyond to buy a meal. Or to stay the night. This really wasn't a very nice spot. However, it was a lot cheaper than anywhere nice. It is also a tribute to the publicans' faith in human greed that they believed people would come if they built a pub there.

Day 157: Levens to Oxenholme
(14 April)

Norwich lost. Of course I wanted them to win but as they lost I was glad I wasn't there.

This time the directions in Levens were so good that I told the woman she should set up an information desk. She said she was used to it because the streets were small and unmarked and all the walkers got lost. She looked elderly (like me) but fit (unlike me) so I asked if she walked or cycled herself. She was rather modest about it so she was probably a world champion.

Four hills lay between me and Oxenholme. As it happened they weren't too bad and I had an hour to spare before my train. I used it constructively by falling asleep in the waiting room.

The politest sixth former in the country was working in the tea rooms at Natland. He was studying Sociology, Eng Lit and one other at A level. He was lucky enough to escape my views on Sociology.

Oxenholme is another dismal place, but it represents a boundary. I hope to strike north and then east from here. I am coming to realise that I have been deluded. I had thought that this was one of the narrow parts of England. I may have got this wrong; in any event it's best not to look at the map too closely in case it is depressing.

But I was back on track.

Day 158: Oxenholme to Killington Lake
(9 May)

Well, I needed a new belt anyway.

I had a bit of work in Birmingham, found that I had forgotten my belt, bought a new one in TK Maxx by New Street station and wondered why all the cheap belts were made for very fat people; this one went round me twice but needed several new holes punching.

I must have looked a rare sight climbing out of Oxenholme in the rain, cup of tea in one hand, pie in the other, trousers round my crotch. I threw away the tea. Then the rain piddled down and I went in a pub for another tea. The landlady made me pay before she would produce the tea.

Oxenholme has one tourist attraction: the pie shop and bakery by the station. I asked how many pies they made in a week. Hundreds. Thousands. Too many to count. They are renowned from Preston to Carlisle. The woman who made my pie said it had real cheese, real onion and real potato in it.

Between the Lake District and the Pennines lies an area that is still pleasant, sometimes beautiful and a great deal cheaper than its fashionable neighbours. Many former workers' cottages have been converted into desirable residences. A high proportion, however, seem to be up for sale. Did they buy them in summer? When winter came, did they think they had made a terrible mistake?

At the top of a long hill I turned to look back at what I had done. Impressive. It was nothing like as impressive, though, as the hills that lay ahead.

Killington Lake is a reservoir with services on the M6. One can eat there all night. Where? McDonald's or, believe it or not, WH Smith. I chose neither but went instead to the petrol station where they heated up a slice of pizza. At least I think it was pizza.

Day 159: Killington to Old Tebay
(10 May)

It was staggering in every sense.

To the east, huge, hulking, magnificent Pennine hills loom over the hastening traveller. To the north, the motorway climbs steadily up the valley of the River Lune until it reaches the bleak and hostile land around Shap.

I had always wanted to walk up this valley. The reality of actually walking it, however, is different from the picture seen from car or train window. Road and rail slide gradually up the valley. The walking route follows an endless series of climbs and descents. After the first couple, the climbs came a few steps at a time; then a halt; then another few steps. I am due to have my heart procedure in July. That's a bit late for this business.

Outside my window this morning a goldcrest was busy on the grass. Later a buzzard hovered over me, which I thought was unfriendly. I had to walk back round the lake; it's always annoying to cover the ground twice. Then it was off towards Lowgill, a viaduct for the Lune Valley Railway, and a signpost for the last five miles to Tebay. Or six to Old Tebay.

A couple stopped their car to see if I was all right. We chatted. The woman's father has nearly completed the Wainwrights: that is, all the tops above a certain height in the Lake District. She has done a number of them with him. We chatted some more. When I found myself talking about Patrick Leigh Fermor, whom they had not heard of, I realised I was becoming a garrulous old man. In exchange for their kindness I offered to buy them a coffee in Tebay motorway services, where I was being picked up at 4.30, if they were in the area.

Fortunately it was a loose arrangement. I never made Tebay services. I hope they didn't go there.

Tebay itself was, I am afraid, not very memorable except for the very helpful pedestrians. It lies at the edge of one of the supposed gaps in the Pennines. The theory is that I will zoom north-eastwards towards my remaining destinations.

And there in Old Tebay, waiting to help me do so, were Companion and dog! Both, it has to be said, were very patient.

The scenery was just magnificent. If I hadn't been walking round the letter Qs I would never have seen all this.

Day 160: Tebay to Ravenstonedale
(12 May)

Never leave it four days before you write up your account. I can't remember a thing about this bit.

I do remember the toast. A faint brown tinge suggested that it had definitely made the acquaintance of the toaster, probably at a distance of a couple of feet. The beans were lukewarm and so was the tea. The venue had better be nameless but it was the only one en route.

We talked about walking for pleasure once all this is over. Not only do I not remember what it is like to walk for pleasure but I can't do it anyway. Until my heart at least is sorted out I can't even look at a hill. I come to a halt after a few paces. There is not much pleasure in that.

There seem to be a lot of places called Newbiggin but this one is distinguished by being Newbiggin-on-Lune. These villages used to have facilities: shops, pubs, a post office, even a bank. Now the houses look nice but the villages are sterile.

There, that has filled up some of the space. The road undulated, I remember that. The scenery remained great. Thassit.

We talked about the next stage. From Ravenstonedale the road climbs a very, very steep hill. My Companion suggested I used some of my banked miles to fly (figuratively) over this section. Planning a route over the next bit is difficult.

Day 161: Along the A66
(13 May)

I could leave this for a decade and still remember every detail of the day. Unfortunately.

We decided to jump ahead. The notorious A66, usually blocked in winter, was wild and woolly at any time. My Companion dropped me at the junction with the old road through Barras. I would come back and fill in the gaps later.

On the map a public footpath ran along the route of an old railway line to the south of the main road. I set off cheerfully. The path grew bigger. It was indeed the dismantled route of an old line. The walking was a piece of cake and no-one was about. Why was it so beautiful but completely deserted?

There was a reason.

It wasn't the bull in the herd of cows. He observed me without interest as I pretended to be invisible and slunk away. The first few gates opened without a problem and closed behind me. Then the gates grew harder and were padlocked and I had to climb over a few. The wildlife was astonishing: ducks, geese, curlews, peewits, grouse, a stoat, two herds of deer and then a massive bird. Could it possibly have been an eagle? A farmer later said it must have been a buzzard and he may have been right, but it was a very big buzzard.

Oh, and a million rabbits.

An even higher and harder gate blocked the path. I looked around but the only option was over the top. I went for it.

And got stuck.

I couldn't even identify what I was stuck by. Something was stopping me getting down the other side. I twisted, turned and wriggled to no avail. Was it my trousers that were caught, or my boots? I tried to stretch down from my horizontal position to free myself. Same outcome. Totally stuck.

Carrion. They would start circling soon. Nobody would come along here for days.

After fifteen minutes things were desperate. I managed to reach my bootlace, loosened the top of the boot and yanked hard. One of the hooks broke off completely. Another was twisted beyond use. I didn't care. I was free.

I carried on but was beginning to get the message about access. A bit further down the path, a very large notice warned that the fence across the track was fired with 5,000 volts. I got the distinct impression that the landowner didn't entertain visitors. Turning at right angles, I staggered up the hill to the main road. The farmer came out to see if I was all right. I assured him I was; then I got the first word in before he could. 'I'm sorry I was on your land.' True. 'I thought it was a public footpath,' I said. True.

'It's not.'

'I came off as soon as I realised it wasn't.' Also true.

He was dour but he was all right. We chatted dourly. How many sheep did he have? 'Two thousand mebbe.' How did he turn right on the A66? He turns left and travels a mile and a half before he can turn.

'Don't try crossing it. They'll wipe you out.'

It seemed a very long way to the junction for Barnard Castle. Companion and dog were waiting. They had nearly become a mountain rescue team.

Day 162: Kirkby Stephen to Barras and back
(25 May)

The previous two days had kept me limbered up just in getting here.

Colin dropped me at the bus stop three miles away from home. As he drove away, I realised I had left my keys on the kitchen table; so I had to walk back and get them.

Yesterday I travelled to Manchester for a meeting in the morning and another meeting in the afternoon. I was scheduled for the 4.56 to Leeds for Kirkby Stephen. I arrived at Piccadilly station at about four o'clock and made enquiries.

'I don't know if you can get to Kirkby Stephen today,' she said.

What?

There was a strike. The only option was to travel to the other end of the line, Carlisle, and come back.

The interval between trains in Carlisle was twelve minutes. Hmm. I got on the Carlisle train. Halfway through the journey, we were running ten minutes late. I asked the guard if he could ring ahead to hold the next train till I got there. He refused. 'They won't hold it,' he said.

As I ran over the footbridge at Carlisle, my train pulled out.

'Of course we'd have held it,' said the staff member in the station. 'Did you ask?'

'Yes.'

'Come with me.'

He sat me down in the office while his colleague rang the other train company and told them what their employee had done - or not done. They sanctioned a taxi to Kirkby Stephen. Forty-seven miles. Each way.

It turned out that I had been to the area of Turkey that the taxi driver came from. We chatted about Carlisle, which he loves, and Leytonstone where we have both worked. I was able to advise on official agencies that he had need of. He was mild mannered in every way but he had one regular expression which he used very frequently to express surprise, shock, anger, solidarity or pleasure. It was two words and they began with F and H.

I was looking forward to Kirkby Stephen. It proved to be scenic but eccentric.

I could not have anticipated starting my time there with an erudite discussion on crime fiction with Nick, who with his partner Rachel runs the excellent Old Croft guesthouse. They have a good collection of crime novels and know what they're talking about. And, like any good aficionado, if there is a bad book on the shelves they say someone else left it there.

(They don't mess about, Rachel and Nick. When they say breakfast is between 8.00 and 8.30, don't expect a piece of toast at 8.45. By 9.30 they want to be heading for the hills and they expect all their guests to be wanting the same.)

Nor could I have expected a long conversation in the pub with Nathan the barman and his mum the cook about films. It was quiet in the pub because it was quiz night - in the other pub across the road. At quiz time everyone, including the landlord and landlady, moved across the road to take part. When it was over they came back again.

Among the customers were some contractors who had been staying there for a while. One of them thought he would have a night off the booze. While I was watching he had four pints of blackcurrant cordial. Outside in the takeaway, everyone seemed to be ordering veggie burgers. Big husky men too. I am not alone.

Showing the business acumen for which the area is famous, both chip shops were closed on a Thursday.

So in the morning I set off promptly, on eviction from the guesthouse, to cover the link road to the nightmare stretch where I got gate-tied. No, I wasn't going to walk the bit before Kirkby Stephen because I had already done the equivalent. What's more, I would punish myself today so heavily that no-one could criticise my pusillanimity.

I walked there and back again.

Barras scarcely exists. Nowhere along the route was there a pub, a shop or anywhere else I could buy an ice cream. Instead there were steep hills.

Very steep hills.

You don't often get asked to walk (or drive) up twenty per cent hills. That's one in five! That was the steepest but there were others not far behind. It was, I thought, pretty valiant of me to walk straight back again. I turned down a lift on a tractor and reached Winton where I was picked up not only by my Companion and the dog but Jamie too.

The highlight of the day? As I was leaning against a gate, searching the map for something or other, a weasel scuttled past my feet.

Day 163: Bowes to Staindrop
(27 May)

The best gin for making damson gin is Sainsbury's own brand. Not the bottom priced Essentials but the next one up. If you buy a litre and a half it works out cheaper than Essentials too.

How do I know all this? (And much, much more.) Wisdom on this and other topics (straining, draining, bottling) was dispensed by the young woman in the tourist shop at Barnard Castle, along with cups of tea and ice cream.

This is a pleasant tourist town. Inevitably it is up a hill. Day trippers thronged the streets. Nothing the matter with that. I was hoping to reach Bishop Auckland on the second day so I pressed on; I might as well have hung about and done a bit of thronging.

The day started badly. Despite all our experience, my Companion and I set off on a footpath. It led nowhere, of course, and was too overgrown for the dog to be visible. We gave up. Then they went off and I headed for Bishop Auckland.

By the time I got to Staindrop I was in no shape to go anywhere. The road was busy and the verges were high. Each time a vehicle passed, I had to get off the road. To get off the road I had to take a giant's step upwards. It was very good exercise for a giant but I couldn't walk any further. I went to the pub and waited for the bus to Darlington.

Like most people, I have been through Darlington on the train many times but have never disembarked. (Belgium used to be the same.) Now I found that the town is entirely given over to festival. Is it always like this? Is life in Darlington one long party? Will I ever come back to it to find out?

I bought some cheese from a farmer who is probably still talking about the methods of production. Hundreds of revellers covered the rest of the city centre. For revellers they were very quiet.

In Darlington at breakfast (help yourself from the cupboard) I met a man who had been competing in Formula B and a woman who was going off to see her grandchild. 'You can't be old enough to have grandchildren,' I said with the gallantry that seemed to be expected. 'Of course I am,' she replied. 'I'm thirty-eight!'

Now the question. How exactly did Staindrop get its name? Is it very embarrassing to say you come from there?

Day 164: Staindrop to Bishop Auckland
(28 May)

A flashing blue light went at speed in the opposite direction. Then another one. There must be an accident somewhere. At least they weren't after me this time.

Two minutes later...

Officer 2960 couldn't have been more reasonable. Someone had rung in to say that some old git was walking 'unsteadily' down the road wearing a red coat and carrying a green rucksack, a well-known offence.

'Red coat and green rucksack,' said 2960. 'That looks like you.'

We agreed on that one.

'I'd guess everything's all right?'

We agreed on that one too.

I sat in the car and we had a chat. He offered water and a ride, both of which I graciously declined. When I told him what I was doing he asked if he would be in the book; I assured him he would. He suggested I write his number on my hand lest I forget it. I gave him a brief rundown on Bishop Auckland football in the 1950s, which I am sure he was grateful for. Then he went back to work.

Of course he took my basic details. If you ask them the way to the bus station they want to know your date of birth. I don't mind. What would be good though would be if people came and had a word with me before ringing the police to say I am unsteady.

The funny thing was that on re-starting the walk I was off like a rat out of a trap. Speed, posture, heads up - all of them were superb for a couple of miles when the officer might be looking. Maybe I don't look right all the time but there are times when surely - surely - I must look normal?

The day's walking began at Staindrop. Heading north out of town the land seemed to widen out like the open spaces of *The Go-Between*. What were we coming to?

Wow. That's quite a castle.

Raby Castle is still very much inhabited. It's also rather beautiful. If I was ever inclined to come back this way, I might go and have a look at it.

Bishop Auckland bus station after six o'clock at night is slightly less lively than the morgue.

Days 165-166: QUARRINGTON HILL, QUEBEC, QUAKING HOUSES
(13-15 June)

AND THAT'S IT!

There was a plan.

For the last couple of days I was going to base myself in the Travelodge in Durham and go out each day. On the first day, for example, I would catch the bus to Bishop Auckland, where I had finished before, and walk to Quarrington Hill. Or Quebec. Or any bloody place.

Hector put paid to that one.

Storm Hector brought the strongest winds ever measured in Britain in June. They blew all night and they blew all morning and it didn't seem a good idea to go out walking. By the afternoon things had abated sufficiently that I only occasionally got blown over, so I walked to Quebec from the city centre.

In Durham market place, volunteers were public spiritedly giving out tourist advice. What's more, they were giving out good advice. Having told me I had chosen three highly unmemorable hamlets to visit, they gave superb walking instructions to all of them.

First came a bridleway along a former railway line (legal, without gate traps), a lovely walk heavily populated with other walkers. This led to the vibrant small town of Langley Park and ultimately, up a considerable hill, to the very quiet village of Quebec. I already had several extra miles in reserve and I added to them through the walk back down from Quebec to Langley Park.

What a nice county this is! I had imagined the frozen north, barren and hostile. Actually the vast majority of it is soft and verdant. And hilly. It could pass for Sussex.

Then there is the city, which has most things you could want: castle, cathedral, university, prison. Just beware of the café in the market hall, where one member of staff will overcharge you if she can.

I took a taxi up to Quarrington Hill and walked back down. As a contrast with my market hall experience I had very cheap beans on toast in a café. Then a man came in after me and also had beans on toast but added an extra slice of toast and three poached eggs and she charged him only another 70p! It was worth going to Durham to see.

Finally - finally - the fatigue comes back on thinking about it - I used my reserve miles to take a bus to Stanley and walk up to Quaking Houses. From twin villages at Quaking Houses two hundred miners were killed in the First World War.

Quaking Houses now sustains neither a mine nor a shop nor a pub. They tried to run a community shop but it floundered. Let's hope the gym does better. In the community hall they were preparing for an event on Sunday. They took photos of us all which I hope will reach me one day. It was a good way to end.

And that is indeed the end...

Oh, my Companion is called Hilary.

Also by Jeremy Cameron

Never Again
A Walk from Hook of Holland to Istanbul

ISBN: 9781908493965

Elderly British men display a variety of annoying habits. They write letters to the newspapers; they drink too much; they reminisce about the old days; they make lewd comments to younger women; they shout at the television screen; and they go for long walks and get lost.

Jeremy Cameron chose the last of these options. Trying to emulate Patrick Leigh Fermor's feat of 1933, he walked from Hook of Holland to Istanbul.

The main point of travel is to recognise the virtues of staying at home. When at home, it is not possible to get bogged down in Alpine snow, fall over on one's face on Kosovan tarmac or suffer a comprehensive mugging on deserted roads in Greece. Nor does one have to speak foreign languages, eat foreign food or, above all, drink terrible tea.

"Cameron writes with one hand wired to the mains."—*Literary Review*